Leaps and Boundaries

The Prayer Book
in the 21st Century

Paul V. Marshall
and Lesley A. Northup, editors

Morehouse Publishing
P.O. Box 1321
Harrisburg, PA 17105

A catalog record for this book is available from the Library of Congress.

ISBN: 0-8192-1718-2

Printed in the United States of America.

Table of Contents

Leaping Beyond the Bonds of Boundaries

Preface

Ritual action is a means by which its participants discover who they are in the world and "how it is" with the world. If we concentrate attention on ritual as an entirely fixed and unvarying sequence of actions, we are likely to overlook this aspect of ritual knowledge altogether.[1]

LITURGY NEVER REMAINS STATIC, nor should it. It is a fond illusion that our rites are timeless, immutable, divinely ordained. While we may ascribe to them a core of timeless meaning, their performance, regulation, form, arrangement, and use have always been in flux, responding to the movement of human thought, understanding, evolution, and need. Liturgy has no existence beyond the persons who enact and enable it; as those persons change and grow, as their cultures wax and wane, so too do the rituals that express their deepest understanding of their relationship with God and the Church.

Were it not so, we could all be attending services in which priests, speaking in dead languages, make up eucharistic prayers as they go along, while the unbaptized (that is, those not immersed in the river) leave before the recitation of the Creed and women are enjoined to remain silent. Were it not so, we could be muttering solitary prayers to the Virgin while the clergy, hidden behind a screen, reserve the communion for themselves. Were it not so, we might be receiving the eucharist but once a year (if then), enduring two-hour sermons, and stripping our churches of all ornamentation.

   This continual alteration is also reflected in prayer book evolution. A brief historical review confirms that the Book of Common Prayer in the Anglican/Episcopal line has been revised officially seven times since its first appearance in 1549; moreover, numerous serious attempts at revisions—for example, in 1689 and, in America, in 1785—failed at adoption but nonetheless exercised considerable influence on liturgical development. Perhaps even more telling are the uncountable small adjustments made to the practice of liturgy in the interstices between formal revisions—every General Convention has made some change or another to the liturgical life of the Church in response to shifting norms, newly recognized needs, and alterations in the Church's understanding and expression of itself. We tend to see the issuance of new prayer books as great divides—Big Moments—but they are not. They are merely way stations in the progress of the Church, fault lines along with the accumulating stresses of cultural, psychological, and theological change moved more dramatically than usual.

These shifts are inevitably accompanied by controversy. And that, too, is as it should be. While liturgy must and will change, it should not be altered hastily or without due consideration. Debate and discussion are crucial to the formation of some consensus on the ritual of the church. Many reading these lines will snort at the implication that liturgical change represents any kind of common consent. But the relatively quick acceptance of each succeeding prayer book indicates that, in almost every case, the broad majority of the faithful have found the new rites a meaningful and effective path to spiritual communion.

Liturgical controversy evokes new ideas, encourages experiment, provokes dialogue, freshens perspectives, and stimulates discovery. It is not to be feared or shunned; it is neither dangerous nor un-Christian. Ideally, it should occur outside the auspices of official ecclesiastical agencies, which by their nature must be conservative. It should lift up the voices of all the Church, using the liturgical expertise of the worshipper and the scholar, the musician and the bishop, the deacon and the acolyte, the altar guild member and the chorister, the celebrant and the usher, the child and the adult.

Jennings, in the epigraph above, focuses our attention on the way in which ritual not only provides a familiar avenue to communication with both the transcendent and immanent expressions of God but also tells us who we are in the world in which we live and in the world of the divine. We have often heard it said that how we worship shapes what we believe; more critically, it also shapes who we are, both individually and as a community. It tells us our place in the plan, directs our activities, gives us an identity. As we change, either as persons or as a Church, our ritual life must also change if it is to reflect the truth about who we are and what we believe. At times, when we are most inspired, the changes may not just reflect the truth but also make it come to be so. Our liturgical life does not happen in a vacuum; as symbolic expression it both points to and effects a deeper reality. Changing our communal prayer is not merely a matter of "updating," of being trendy or relevant; it also involves a redefinition of who and what we are as Church and of our role in the culture around us.

The various contributors to this volume were approached with the invitation to discuss the liturgy and the possibilities for altering it from the boundaries, the assumed demarcations that we traditionally place around our liturgical life to protect it from incautious change. They were further invited to leap those boundaries and consider points of view not likely to get a hearing in officially authorized forums. Some have done that with daring; others have chosen a more Anglican via media; still others have chosen a conservative approach. In this, they represent the kind of dialectic that must always accompany liturgical reconsideration.

Marion Hatchett's chapter on "unfinished business" sets the stage with numerous suggestions that would strengthen the current prayer book, reduce misunderstanding, and correct bizarre new practices. Two contributors offer observations on aspects of our worship life all too often ignored when revision is discussed. Carol Doran reflects on the role of music in liturgical renewal, urging a fuller exploration of its potential to enhance worship and build faith. Leigh Axton Williams draws a connection between liturgy and the instrument through which it is so often altered—canon law—suggesting a fresh approach aimed at elevating our appreciation of these interrelated aspects of our ecclesiastical life.

The rites of initiation—and the wrongs that accompany them—are addressed by Paul Marshall, who catalogs the liturgical disasters that have crept into our practice as we misunderstand the relationship of liturgy and culture. A similar concern is identified by Linda Moeller, who spotlights the current debate about open table fellowship, considering the historical and theological factors that affect the topic. Another form of initiation is discussed by Richard Leggett, who suggests important adjustments in the rite for consecrating a bishop. And Ormonde Plater looks closely at the functions of the deacon in the liturgy, proposing numerous changes that challenge the Church to clearly define and unashamedly incorporate the deacon's role in worship.

A final set of chapters makes suggestions that may startle some readers but may also open the door for a more rigorous and courageous look at our liturgy. In light of the current debate about full intercommunion, Philip Pfatteicher discusses the possibilities for a prayer book that "works" for both Episcopalians and Lutherans. Paul Marshall challenges easy assumptions about emotion in worship, defining ecstasy available to worshippers who look beyond, not merely within, for liturgical spirituality. Lesley Northup suggests that we may have something to learn from feminist liturgical experimentation. Finally, Neil Alexander's chapter proposes the reconsideration of some basic principles of prayer book worship that have long been held to be inviolate, while posing more general questions about the principles that should underlie further revision as the Church moves into the twenty-first century.

Liturgy never remains static, nor should it. To the extent that it does, so do we. This small volume throws down a preliminary gauntlet to those discussing liturgical revision: Are we, it asks, prepared to change the liturgy and let it change us? Are we open to seeing the liturgy as our self-expression and the self-expression of the Church and open to considering change in light of what we believe we are about? Can we go beyond mere liturgical tinkering and tackle the big, difficult questions? Are we willing to leap the boundaries set by our liturgical ancestors and forge new habits of thought and action to guide the worship of the twenty-first century?

Paul V. Marshall
Bethlehem, Pennsylvania
February 1997

Lesley A. Northup
Miami, Florida
February 1997

Contributors

J. Neil Alexander is the Trinity Church Professor of Liturgics and Preaching in the General Theological Seminary, New York City. His published works include *Time and Community*.

Carol Doran is Assistant Professor of Church Music and Director of Community Worship at Colgate/Rochester/Bexley Hall, New York.

Marion J. Hatchett is Professor of Liturgy and Church Music at the School of Theology of the University of the South. He served on drafting committees for the eucharist, the lectionary, and the rubrics of the *1979 Book of Common Prayer*, and on the text and Anglican chant committees for the *Hymnal 1982*. Among his books are *A Commentary on the American Prayer Book* and *Sanctifying Life, Time, and Space*.

Richard G. Leggett is Assistant Professor of Liturgics at Vancouver School of Theology in British Columbia.

Paul V. Marshall is bishop of the Episcopal Diocese of Bethlehem and former Associate Professor of Liturgics at Yale University Divinity School. His books include the multi-volume *Prayer Book Parallels*.

Linda Moeller is completing Th.D. studies in liturgics at the General Theological Seminary, concentrating on the sacraments of initiation.

Lesley A. Northup is Assistant Professor of Religion and Culture at Florida International University in Miami. Her books include *Women and Religious Ritual* and *The 1892 Book of Common Prayer*.

Philip H. Pfatteicher is Professor of English at East Stroudsburg in Pennsylvania and has written the authoritative commentaries on the *Lutheran Book of Worship.*

Ormonde Plater is the leading authority on the diaconate in the Episcopal Church. His writings include the classic *The Deacon in the Liturgy.*

Leigh Axton Williams, a practicing attorney, is completing Th.D. studies at the General Theological Seminary in the field of canon law.

The Big Picture

Unfinished Business in Prayer Book Revision

Marion J. Hatchett

I AM SURE THAT NONE OF US who worked on drafting committees for the various rites of the *1979 Book of Common Prayer* saw that book as finished, completed. Many issues had been raised that were considered inexpedient pastorally (a high sounding word that often really means *politically*) to deal with at that time. Deletion of certain old forms and terms might have resulted in the defeat of the book. Certain rubrics were deliberately made ambiguous. Certain things were implied but, for political reasons, not spelled out.

The rubrics committee operated on certain assumptions that at the time seemed reasonable to us: that clergy, church musicians, and others responsible for ordering worship can read *italics*; that they will read the rubrics; that they will read the book through from cover to cover; and that they will compare the rubrics of this book carefully with those of prior prayer books and with the various trial rites that had been in use and they will realize that, when the book opts for certain things, it is opting against alternative interpretations or practices. Also, we did not recognize the need to include in the book definitions of some liturgical terms (for example, *Salutation, Grace, Chrism, Charge*).

OTHER RECENT LITURGICAL BOOKS

WHAT IS SOMETIMES still referred to as "the new prayer book" is now an old book among Anglican prayer books and among the worship books of mainline denominations in America.

Since the ratification of the *Book of Common Prayer 1979* (BCP 79), at least eight Anglican prayer books have been published in the English language:

ASB

The Alternative Service Book 1980: Services authorized for use in the Church of

England in conjunction with the Book of Common Prayer (Clowes; SPCK; Cambridge Univ. Press, 1980)

IRE
Alternative Prayer Book 1984 according to the use of the Church of Ireland (London: Collins Liturgical Publications, 1984)

CW
The Book of Common Prayer for use in the Church in Wales (Church in Wales Publications, 1984)

BAS
The Book of Alternative Services of the Anglican Church of Canada (Toronto: Anglican Book Centre, 1985); also see *Occasional Celebrations of the Anglican Church in Canada* (1992)

SA
An Anglican Prayer Book 1989: Church of the Province of South Africa (London: Collins Liturgical Publications, 1989)

NZ
A New Zealand Prayer Book (Auckland: Collins, 1989)

Aus
A Prayer Book for Australia (Broughton Books, 1995)

WI
The Book of Common Prayer: The Church in the Province of the West Indies (New York: Church Hymnal Corporation, 1996)

Since the approval of the first reading in 1976 of the *Proposed Book of Common Prayer*, several other worship books have been published in American mainline denominations, including the following:

LBW
Lutheran Book of Worship (Minneapolis: Augsburg Publishing House; Philadelphia: Board of Publication, Lutheran Church in America, 1978);

see also *Lutheran Book of Worship: Ministers Desk Edition* (1978) (LBW:MDE) and *Occasional Services: A Companion to the Lutheran Book of Worship* (1982)

UMBW
The United Methodist Book of Worship (Nashville: United Methodist Publishing House, 1992)

BCW
Book of Common Worship: Prepared by the Theology and Worship Ministry Unit for the Presbyterian Church (U.S.A.) and the Cumberland Presbyterian Church (Louisville: Westminster/John Knox Press, 1993)

Some of these books have incorporated material from BCP 79, and other revisions have incorporated new or recovered earlier theological and liturgical thinking, and have dared to spell out things that for pastoral or political reasons had to be made ambiguous or could only be implied in BCP 79.

The first *Book of Common Prayer* of 1549 established a style that has generally been maintained in subsequent revisions: the 1549 rubrics were stated in positive terms—certain things were to be done or may be done; only rarely was an action forbidden. The exception in 1549 was that the Institution Narrative was "to be said, turning still to the Altar, without any elevacion or shewing the Sacrament to the people." Should future revisions contain more equivalent rubrics that forbid certain actions, since it is obvious that many people making decisions do not seem to have been adequately prepared to draw conclusions from omissions or implications?

MATTERS OF LAYOUT AND TERMINOLOGY
HYMNAL REVISION ENCOUNTERED MUCH LESS RESISTANCE than prayer book revision probably because everyone realized the hymnal had been frequently revised. After all, it had 1940 printed on its title page. A revision of the *Book of Common Prayer* should have the date of its adoption printed on its title page and on its cover, as do some of the other recent Anglican revisions (ASB 1980, Ire 1984, SA 1989).

In "The Collects for the Church Year" (p. 157-261) and in "The

Lectionary" (p. 887-1001), we should for clarity follow the practice of BAS, Aus and BCW in designating collects and lections for ordinary time ("Week following Sunday between June 12 and 18 inclusive" rather than "Week of the Sunday closest to June 15"). In "The Collects for the Church Year" and in "The Lectionary" the propers should be numbered from the First Sunday after the Epiphany rather than from the Sunday closest to May 11 (see BAS and Aus).

Few congregations seem to have been well instructed about joining in on unison forms, and these forms often begin in a very ragged, ugly manner. Some books (including LBW) have printed the first line of these forms in a different style from the lines to be said in unison, and this certainly makes for a more unified and attractive beginning of unison forms.

Should we not follow the lead of ASB, Ire, CW, BAS, SA, NZ, Aus, WI, LBW, UMBW, and BCW (that is, all eleven of the books listed above) in printing congregational responses and prayers in **bold** type?

Wherever they appear, the Apostles' and Nicene creeds should be printed with a colon after the first line ("I believe in God:" or "We believe in God:") with the congregation joining in on the second line, which should begin "the Father...."

We need to find convenient one, two, or three syllable names for "An Order for Celebrating the Holy Eucharist" (often called "Rite Three") and for the "Liturgy of the Word of God with Administration of the Holy Communion from the Reserved Sacrament" (often called a "deacon's mass"). These commonly used terms are misleading. The first of these services is not a "rite," for it consists of a series of rubrics rather than texts, and the second is not a "mass" but a form for administering "Communion under Special Circumstances."

Print some Additional Directions as rubrics within the rites and relegate some texts to Additional Directions (see below).

In the rubrics, print the words "may" and "or" in bold print. (I was present at one service in which we got all three Opening Acclamations followed by the Collect for Purity, the Gloria in excelsis, the Kyrie in English, the Kyrie in Greek and the Trisagion. I was glad that all six forms of the Prayers of the People and all four forms of the Eucharistic Prayer were not printed *in situ*.)

The layout of the book assumes that people will realize that when the *Amen* is printed in italics and the prayer is not printed in sense lines (that is, arranged so that the congregation will keep together by breathing at the end of each line—the way the Nicene Creed and the Confession of Sin are laid out in the eucharistic rites), the intention is that the prayer be said by the celebrant alone with the people's participation consisting of listening to the celebrant and expressing their assent by saying, "Amen" (see pp. 282, 399, 432, 457, 482-98, 535, and 546-47). The rubric prior to the form should state clearly that the prayer is to be said by the celebrant alone. On the other hand, when the intention is that the form be said by all, the text should be printed in sense lines and the Amen in the same typeface as the text (see pp. 308, 522, and 564).

It is confusing (and often embarrassing) to people when, in services that they seldom attend, they confront the short form of the Lord's Prayer (pp. 106, 132-33, 153, and 464). When the Kyrie precedes the Lord's Prayer, it will be the short form; this is a bit of gnosis that feeds the pride of some people but creates a situation that embarrasses many. BCP 79 added the doxology to the short form of the Lord's Prayer in the Committal of the burial rite. It should be added in these other occasional rites as well.

The latest form of the International Consultation on English in the Liturgy (ICEL) texts should be used for all of the "common" texts. Some of the newer books print only the ICEL form of the Lord's Prayer, and that should be considered.

CONCERNING THE SERVICE OF THE CHURCH

WI ADDS THIS SENTENCE TO THE FIRST RUBRIC: "It is the duty of every member of the Church to be present at the Holy Eucharist every Sunday, and on other Holy Days, according to opportunity."

Hymns is defined; should *anthems* also be defined? Ire contains a sentence that perhaps should be added to this rubric: "In the selection of hymns [and anthems] careful attention should be given to see that they are appropriate to the theme of the Bible readings and sermon."

Revise the last of these paragraphs to substitute the New Revised Standard Version of the Bible (NRSV) as the source of scriptural citations, except for the Psalms.

THE CALENDAR OF THE CHURCH YEAR

IN "THE CALENDAR OF THE CHURCH YEAR," should there be more flexibility about days on which Epiphany or Ascension are celebrated? Falling on odd days, the attendance is often much smaller than at regularly scheduled weekday services. Should Transfiguration take precedence over Sunday on August 6 (which interrupts the course readings) when we have the account of the Transfiguration as the Gospel every year on the Last Sunday after the Epiphany?

Should Red Letter Days (with the possible exception of Annunciation [and St. Joseph?]) be transferred out of Advent and Lent as in the current Roman calendar and a number of Anglican calendars? In ASB and BAS, St. Thomas is to be commemorated on July 3; in SA, NZ, Aus and WI, it may be celebrated on that date. In ASB, BAS, and SA, St. Matthias is to be commemorated on May 14; in Aus and WI, it may be celebrated on that date. In BAS, SA, NZ, Aus, and WI, St. Stephen and St. John are moved to August 3 and May 6, respectively. In BAS and SA, Holy Innocents may be moved to January 11; in NZ, it may be moved to February 16. BAS and WI states, "When the feasts of Saint Joseph or the Annunciation fall on a Sunday in Lent they are transferred to the preceding Saturday or to a day in the preceding weeks." Should we follow their lead? In a similar vein, should St. Andrew's Day be celebrated in the preceding week when the First Sunday in Advent falls on November 29 or November 30?

The BCP 79 simply states that the Ember Days have traditionally been observed on certain dates; the intention is that they may now be observed at other times, most suitably in weeks that precede diocesan ordinations. The rubric in NZ and Aus evidently has some such thing in mind: "Prayers are offered on the weekdays following the Day of Pentecost and the week preceding St. Andrew's Day."

Suggest that appropriate observances of Rogation Days have a relationship to local times of planting, etc. NZ, Aus, and WI direct that the Rogation Days be observed at times when crops are planted.

Most of the more recent books have used one or both of two titles for the Last Sunday after Pentecost: Christ the King or The Reign of Christ.

THE DAILY OFFICE
Daily Morning and Evening Prayer

In addition to the traditional Anglican Daily Offices of Morning and Evening Prayer, which are based largely on monastic offices, BCP 79 includes "An Order of Worship for the Evening," which is a type that has come to be called a "cathedral" office. Do we not also need an equivalent morning office? Such an office is well suited for a congregation mostly made up of people who do not participate regularly in Daily Morning or Evening Prayer. Such an office would have the flexibility of the orders for eucharist, marriage, and burial. BCW provides an outline for such a morning office.

An Outline of Morning Prayer:

Opening Sentences
Morning Psalm or Morning Hymn
Psalm(s)
    Psalm
    Silent Prayer
    [Psalm Prayer]
Scripture Reading
    Silent Reflection
    [A Brief Interpretation of the Reading,
    or a Nonbiblical Reading]
Canticle
    Song of Zachariah or Other Canticle
Prayers of Thanksgiving and Intercessions
    Thanksgivings and Intercessions
    Concluding Prayer
    Lord's Prayer
[Hymn or Spiritual]
Dismissal
    [Sign of Peace]

The rubric just before the Confession of Sin in both Daily Morning and Evening Prayer should read "Silence is kept" rather than "Silence may be kept." Despite the fact that within the text the longer forms of the

Exhortation call for a silence, a silence is sometimes not observed.

The book should include additional Invitatories at both Morning and Evening Prayer. BAS suggests that Psalm 24, Ps. 51:1-18, Ps. 63:1-8, Ps. 67, or Ps. 145 may be used as an Invitatory at Morning Prayer; BCW includes Ps. 63:1-8 and Ps. 51:1-12 among the Invitatories at Morning Prayer. It might be suggested that a portion of Psalm 51 is suitable in Lent or on Fridays in Lent. ASB, BAS, SA, Aus, and UMBW all include Psalm 134 for use as an Invitatory in Evening Prayer. Aus, LBW, UMBW, and BCW all include selected verses of Psalm 141 as an Invitatory at Evening Prayer; LBW follows it with a Psalm Prayer. BCP 79 allows use of the Invitatory Psalms from Morning Prayer at Evening Prayer; ASB, CW, Ire, BAS, NZ, Aus, and WI allow the use of the Pascha nostrum at Evening Prayer.

BAS allows use of a hymn in place of an Invitatory Psalm; WI allows a hymn before the variable Psalms, and LBW allows a hymn after the Psalms before the Lesson(s).

"An Order of Worship for the Evening" in BCP 79 provides for silence or a suitable collect, or both, to follow the Psalmody. This provision might also be brought into Morning and Evening Prayer. BAS, LBW:MDE, and BCW all provide a complete series of Psalter collects; Aus provides a selection.

The number of canticles was substantially increased in BCP 79. More than forty other canticles are included in one or more of the recent books. Among those that appear in several books are The Song of Hannah (1 Sam. 2:1-8), God's Chosen One (Isa. 11:1-4,6,7), The Desert Shall Blossom (Isa. 35:1,2,5,6,10), He was Despised and Rejected (Isa. 53:3-5 or 6), The Spirit of the Lord (Isa. 61:1-3,10,11), The Steadfast Love of God (Lam. 3:22-26), The Song of Judith (Jth. 16:13-15), A Song of Wisdom (Wisd. of Sol. 10:15-19, 20b-21), the Beatitudes (Matt. 5:3-12), A Song of Christ's Glory (Phil. 2:6-11), The First-Born of All Creation (Col. 1:15-20), The Mystery of Our Religion (1 Tim. 3:16; 6:15-16), A Song of Christ the Servant (1 Pet. 2:21-24 or 25), A Song of Love (1 John 4:7-6; 1 Cor. 13:4-10, 12-13), and Salvator mundi (Jesus, Savior of the world), written by a nineteenth-century Congregationalist, Dr. Henry Allon.

Should the Great O Advent Anthems [Antiphons] for use with the Magnificat December 17-23 be provided as in SA, LBW, and BCW?

In ancient times the Daily Offices ended with a litany, followed by a collect or prayer and/or the Lord's Prayer, and a Dismissal. The Lord's Prayer was the climax of the prayers rather than an introduction to prayer. This order is recovered in "An Order of Worship for the Evening" in BCP 79 and has been to greater or lesser extents recovered in BAS, NZ, Aus, LBW, UMBW, and BCW. BAS provides a number of litanies for use in the Daily Offices. As in "An Order of Worship for the Evening," permission to exchange the Peace at the conclusion of the rite is provided in UMBW and BCW.

An Order of Service for Noonday

A new title and rubrics for "An Order of Service for Noonday" should indicate that, essentially, we have in this rite materials traditionally used at Terce and Nones, as well as materials used at Sext. So this rite can be adapted to the time of day at which it is used, or it can be used for all three of the traditional Little Offices. "The Divine Office: The Liturgy of the Hours according to the Roman Rite" calls it Prayer During the Day. Might it be called by that title or be called A Little Office or An Office for Use during the Day? BAS and BCW provide for use of Psalm prayers and BAS, NZ, UMBW, and BCW all end the office with intercessions and thanksgivings followed by [a collect and] the Lord's Prayer and a Dismissal.

An Order of Worship for the Evening

In their "Order of Worship for the Evening," BAS, Aus, LBW, and BCW all provide longer Prayers for Light, which are introduced by the dialogue that introduces the Eucharistic Prayers and the Blessing of the Water at baptisms ("Let us give thanks to the Lord our God. **It is right to give our thanks and praise**").

BAS and BCW both provide a "Vigil of the Resurrection" for Saturday evenings, which begins, like their orders of worship for the evening, with an Opening Acclamation, the Phos hilaron, and a Thanksgiving for Light. This is followed by a portion of Psalm 118, a prayer, Psalm 150, one of the Gospel accounts of the Resurrection, a prayer modeled on the Blessing of the Font, the Song of Moses from Exodus 15 (BCW provides the Te Deum as an alternative), a prayer, and an Easter Blessing. BCW suggests that the Thanksgiving over Water be followed by the leader's dipping a hand into the water, lifting up some water, letting it fall back into the font, and then making the sign of the cross over the people while saying,_"Remember your baptism and be thankful." BCW also suggests that, during the singing of the Song of Moses or the Te Deum, all approach the water, dip a hand into it, and "make the sign of the cross, remembering his or her baptism." ASB, NZ, and Aus, though they do not have a Vigil of the Resurrection, suggest or appoint Pascha nostrum for Saturday Evening Prayer.

Daily Evening Prayer
[See Daily Morning and Evening Prayer above]

An Order for Compline
NZ calls it "Night Prayer." Aus titles it "Prayer at the End of the Day also called Compline." LBW and BCW call it "Prayer at the Close of the Day." UMBW calls it "An Order for Night Praise and Prayer".

In "An Order for Compline," a greater number of Psalms and Lessons might be provided. Among Psalms in other books that are not in BCP 79 are 16, 23, 33, 34, 65, 121, 136, and 139:1-12. Among Lessons in other books that are not in BCP 79 are Deut. 6:4-7, Joel 2:28, Matt. 6:31-34, a condensed version of Luke 6:27-38, John 1:4-5, John 14:27, Rom. 8:38-39, 2 Cor. 4:6-10, Eph. 3:15-19, Eph. 4:26-27, 1 Thess. 5:9-10, 1 Thess. 5:23, 2 Tim. 1:7, 1 John 4:18-20, and Rev. 22:3c-5.

As in other offices, the Lord's Prayer might come at the conclusion of the prayers, just before the Nunc dimittis, as it does in LBW, UMBW, and BCW, rather than at the beginning of the prayers.

Print the Antiphon that precedes and follows the Nunc dimittis in sense lines like other unison readings in the book.

ADDITIONAL DIRECTIONS
IT MIGHT BE GOOD to include a direction from LBW:MDE: "Since readings from the Scriptures form a major part of the daily service, a focal center may be created by placing tall, freestanding candlesticks on either side of the lectern or reading desk."

Now that the *Hymnal* has been revised, the permission to use an earlier form of the Gloria Patri (p. 141) should be deleted.

The permission to have a sermon at places other than following the

Lessons (p. 142) should be dropped. Permission to follow the sermon with a period of silence for reflection should be inserted. Drop the bracketed words "[Peace and] Offertory," for permission (p. 407) to have the Peace at a later place.

THE GREAT LITANY

PROVIDE A CONTEMPORARY LANGUAGE FORM of "The Great Litany." Compare those in ASB, Ire, BAS, SA, Aus, WI, LBW, and BCW.

Substitute *humankind* for *mankind* (150, 152-54) and *forbears* for *forefathers* (148) and for fathers (154). Other substitutions might also be considered: "from the cunning assaults of the devil" (WI and LBW) for "from the crafts and assaults of the devil;" "vanity" (ASB, SA, Aus, and WI) for "vainglory;" "From disordered and sinful affections" (SA and WI) for "From all inordinate and sinful affections;" "from the deceits of the world and snares of the devil" (Ire, SA, and WI) for "from all the deceits of the world, the flesh and the devil;" "from epidemic, drought and famine" (LBW) for "from plague, pestilence, and famine;" "In all times of trial and sorrow, in all times of joy and prosperity" (SA and WI) for "in all time of our tribulation; in all time of our prosperity;" "administer justice with mercy" (SA and WI [compare BAS, BCW]) for "do justice, and love mercy;" and "grant to all people freedom and dignity, food and shelter" (SA, WI[compare BAS]) for "and to bestow freedom upon all peoples." On page 154, substitute the current form of Gloria Patri.

After "Baptism, Fasting, and Temptation" add "and by your proclamation of the Kingdom" (BAS, SA, WI, and BCW [compare Ire and Aus: "by your preaching of the Kingdom"]); after "from violence, battle, and murder" add "from corrupt and unjust government" (LBW); after "and that it may please thee to rule and govern thy holy church" add these words: "fill it with love and truth; and grant it that unity which is your will" (ASB, Ire, SA, Aus, WI, and BCW). Add from LBW: "To put an end to all schisms and causes of offense to those who would believe; and to bring into the way of truth...." Add from Aus: "Remember the ancient peoples of this land and forgive the sins of ignorance and neglect done against them." After "give and preserve to our use the bountiful fruits of the earth, so that in due time all may enjoy them," add "help us to use wisely the fruits and treasures of the earth, the sea, and the air" (LBW).

Among the petitions, add "refugees" (ASB, Aus, SA, WI, and BCW), "all who live in fear" (Ire, SA, and WI), "the unemployed" (Ire, BAS, SA, WI, and BCW), "the overworked, the exploited and the oppressed" (SA and WI), "all migrant workers" (SA and WI), for those who have been abused, and for those who abuse.

THE COLLECTS FOR THE CHURCH YEAR

ON PAGE 158, in the second paragraph from the bottom of the page, add from SA: "except that the Collect for Easter Day is not used at Evening Prayer on Holy Saturday."

PROPER LITURGIES FOR SPECIAL DAYS
Ash Wednesday

In the Ash Wednesday rite, print out the Salutation ("The Lord be with you. **And also with you.**"), and print a rubric that says explicitly that this is not to be preceded by a musical prelude or a processional hymn or an Opening Acclamation or the Collect for Purity or Kyrie or Trisagion.

Allow the Psalm (maybe with an Antiphon or Refrain) to begin while ashes are still being imposed.

Allow this Litany of Penitence to be used within "A Penitential Order" in place of the General Confession and Absolution printed there (320/352) on Sundays in Lent. In most places more people come to church on Sundays in Lent than on Ash Wednesday. People need to be exposed to this litany, which is the most penetrating confession of sin that we have ever had in a BCP; it makes a good basis for preparation for "The Reconciliation of a Penitent" or for communion.

Palm Sunday

In the rubrics in the Palm Sunday rite, print the word **branches** in bold print. Follow the lead of LBW:MDE: "The branches are distributed before the service begins." Distributing them after they are blessed is awkward and time consuming.

Should an [optional] introductory address for the Palm Sunday rite be provided, such as that in BAS or the revised version in SA and WI?

In practice, having the congregation take the part of the crowd in the Reading of the Passion causes people to listen for their cue rather than listening to the reading. That permission should be deleted, and clergy should not print in the service sheet, "At the verse which mentions

Golgotha all stand." That, too, causes people to listen for a cue rather than listening to the reading. That rubric should be revised to read: "Before the verse that mentions the arrival at Golgotha, the reader should pause and motion to the congregation to stand."

Maundy Thursday

Should an [optional] introductory address for the Maundy Thursday rite be provided, such as that in BAS or BCW?

Add a rubric from BAS: "The blessing or dismissal may be omitted. The congregation should leave in silence" (compare rubrics in LBW:MDE and BCW).

Should a rubric be inserted, such as that in the Roman Missal, to the effect that, if a watch is kept before the reserved Sacrament, it should be brought to a conclusion no later than midnight?

Good Friday

In regard to the beginning of the Good Friday rite, see Ash Wednesday (above); in regard to the Reading of the Passion, see Palm Sunday (above).

We should adopt the direction of LBW:MDE: "Organ or other instrumental music is used only to support the singing."

The unique optional salutation on Good Friday is awkward; it sends people looking for it in the Prayer Book. It should be detected or the whole (optional) text should be said or sung by the celebrant alone. On the other hand, should the Opening Acclamation of BAS be provided for optional use? If so, should it be read responsively, or simply read by the celebrant or sung by the celebrant or a cantor or the choir?

All we like sheep have gone astray;
we have turned every one to his own way.
And the Lord has laid on him the iniquity of us all.

Christ the Lord became obedient unto death.
Even death on a cross.

Among the rubrics under the reference for the Passion Gospel in WI is this note: "The term 'the Jews' in St. John's Gospel applies to particular individuals and not to the whole Jewish people. Insofar as we ourselves turn against Christ, we are responsible for his death."

The rubric in WI that corresponds to that at the bottom of page 277 contains this sentence: "The silence should be of significant length." If substantial silences are kept during the Solemn Collects, we should follow an ancient tradition in which people stood for collects and biddings and knelt for silences. This is less tiring than either standing or kneeling throughout.

Should the devotions before the cross be headed "Devotions before the Cross," or (as in BAS and WI) "Meditation on the Cross of Jesus," or (as in SA) "The Solemn Adoration of Christ Crucified"?

Consider, as in LBW:MDE, saying or singing at the beginning of the procession, halfway through, and at the altar, "Behold the life-giving cross on which was hung the salvation of the whole world. **Oh, come let us worship him**," or the variation in BCW, "Behold the cross on which was hung the salvation of the whole world. **Come, let us worship**."

The form of the Reproaches in the *Draft Proposed Book of Common Prayer* was rejected at the 1976 General Convention. Consider the form from BAS (which came from an earlier Methodist book and which shows up in revised forms in WI, UMBW, and BCW) or consider the form in SA.

The rubrics certainly imply that there should be no music after the hymn at the end of the devotions before the cross, but this needs to be said explicitly.

A celebration of the eucharist on Good Friday is not explicitly forbidden, and it was commonly done in Anglicanism in earlier times and is still provided for in some of the newer books (BAS, SA, WI). Should there be a rubric (as there is for Holy Saturday) saying, "There is no celebration of the Eucharist on this day"?

Should the Ministration of Holy Communion be given a title?

Some early Sacramentaries said that on Good Friday communion is to be administered in silence. Should this be spelled out in a rubric?

The Good Friday final prayer is printed in a manner that indicates that it is to be said by the celebrant alone with the congregation saying the Amen. The rubric should say, "The celebrant says." Should this concluding prayer be given a title?

Holy Saturday
The Grace needs to be printed out in the Holy Saturday rite. Many people who did not grow up in 1928 Morning Prayer parishes do not know what the word *Grace* in the rubrics of the BCP means.

The Great Vigil of Easter
The rubric on page 286 in the Great Vigil of Easter needs to be expanded to mention the traditional place for the Paschal Candle: "The Paschal Candle is placed in its stand at the pulpit." (I would not have believed it if I had not seen it, but I saw the candle placed in a stand near the altar and the deacon then take out a flashlight in order to be able to sing the Exsultet at the pulpit.) Remove the bars that allow portions of the Exsultet to be omitted. Change the word *man* (p. 287).

People cannot settle into the mood of the vigil with just the required two Lessons. The Romans require at least four. BAS and WT require at least three. SA provides six and requires at least four; a rubric states: "It is desirable that all the readings, with the accompanying psalms and prayers, should be read in their entirety, but for good reason the Third and Fifth Readings and some or all of the psalms may be omitted." LBW provides twelve lections and requires at least seven or four. We should require at least six Lessons with their psalms and prayers. *babies?*

Strike the permission to sing hymns within the Service of Readings. (I have seen service sheets that looked more like Festival Services of Lessons and Carols than like vigils.) The music in this portion of the rite should be restrained. Even canticles might better be sung by a cantor or choir than by the congregation.

The periods of silence and the collects after the Lessons should be obligatory rather than permissive.

If no baptisms are to take place, provide, at the Renewal of Vows, for use of the form for blessing water from the rite "The Dedication and Consecration of a Church," page 570. Provide also for a sprinkling of the people, possibly with the words "Remember your baptism and be thankful" (compare the Vigil of the Resurrection in BCW).[1]

Unfortunately, most congregations do not sing canticles with great gusto. Allow a very popular hymn, such as "Jesus Christ Is Risen Today," after the Easter Acclamation, preceding or taking the place of the canticle. Reverse the order of the canticles listed: Pascha nostrum is a proper

Easter canticle, and the Te Deum at least mentions the Resurrection. Strike from the list the Gloria in excelsis (which does not mention the Resurrection) and substitute the Song to the Lamb.

HOLY BAPTISM AND CONFIRMATION

MAKE THE TEXT of the baptismal and confirmation rites less ambiguous. Go back to the Prayer Book Studies 18.

Under Concerning the Service (p. 298), list prominently the days for which "[it] is recommended that, as far as possible, Baptisms be reserved" (p. 312).

People continue to be caught unawares by the versicles and responses that follow the Opening Acclamation of baptisms or confirmations. It might be better for this passage simply to be read by the celebrant or sung by the celebrant or a cantor or choir. Drop permission to follow these opening versicles with the Gloria (p. 312). That interrupts a more straightforward entrance rite.

Provide within the rite, or in Additional Directions, suitable forms parallel to that provided in the Easter Vigil for introducing the Renewal of Baptismal Vows on the other baptismal occasions.

Consider moving the Affirmation of Faith to just before the water rite, as in most historic baptismal liturgies and in ASB, CW, Ire, BAS, SA, Aus, WI and LBW. In the Prayers for the Candidates, consider substituting the form of the petitions in BAS or in Aus.

Define the word *Chrism*. The word is used several times in BCP 79 but never defined. At the Blessing of Chrism, include a rubric from BAS: "Vessels large enough to be seen clearly by the congregation should be used." Drop the provisions in the *Book of Occasional Services* in which the chrism might be consecrated at the cathedral on Maundy Thursday. State quite explicitly that the chrism should be consecrated in the various parishes at the visitation of the bishop. In this way the people may see the consecration and hear the imagery in the prayer. The anointing with chrism on baptismal occasions will then recall its consecration by the bishop, and the anointing will not come across as the application of a miraculous chapstick sent down from the bishop's office.

Consider including this note from Aus:

Oil may be used if desired at the signing of the cross. The

optional use of oil (chrism) restores an ancient baptismal ceremony. It evokes a rich variety of biblical imagery: the anointing
of kings (1 Samuel 16), the royal priesthood (1 Peter 2), the seal
of the saints (Revelation 7) and is traditionally associated with
the Holy Spirit. Its relationship with the name "Christ," the
anointed one, reminds us that each baptism is related to the
baptism of Jesus.

Consider including this rubric from Aus: "In the celebration of baptism
the symbolism of water should be emphasized. Immersion or the pouring of a significant quantity of water shows this clearly. The pouring of
the water both into the font and over each candidate should be done
deliberately and with care."

Print the form that begins, "We receive you into the household of
God" (p. 308), in sense lines like other unison forms in the book (see BAS).

Drop the use of the name *confirmation* for our rite of Reaffirmation
of Baptismal Vows with Laying on Hands by a Bishop. (This was recommended at the 1974 meeting of chairs of Diocesan Liturgical
Commissions with only one dissenting vote.) What in the BCP tradition
corresponds most closely to the medieval Roman rite of confirmation
(whose sacramental sign is anointing with chrism), and what corresponds most closely to the chrismation in the Eastern rites, is the signa-
tion that follows the baptism with water. The sacramental sign in our rite
of confirmation is not anointing with Chrism but laying on of hands.
Our rite of confirmation can only be administered by a bishop, whereas
in the Eastern rites it is normally administered by a presbyter. In the
Roman rite it may be delegated to a presbyter, and in an emergency it
may be administered by any presbyter not currently under discipline.
We should return to the eighteenth-century Anglican pattern of receiving those baptized in the name of the Trinity who have made an adult
(re)affirmation of faith. Or we should require confirmation of all who
come from any other tradition. The Eastern and Roman churches have
not required an adult reaffirmation of faith, nor is chrismation necessarily administered by a bishop. Those from other traditions (with very few
exceptions) have not, at an affirmation or reaffirmation of faith, received
a laying on of hands by a bishop. Explicitly require the laying on of hands
for those who come for reception and those who come for reaffirmation

as well as for those being "confirmed."

Consider the provisions of SA, The Admission of Baptized Communicants from other Churches into Communicant Membership, or those of Aus, Reception into Communicant Membership. See the rubric in their rite for confirmation: "Baptized communicant members of other churches who wish to be received into communicant membership of this church may be presented to the bishop according to the service of Reception into Communicant Membership." In their rite the order differs from ours; "Confirmation" is immediately followed by reaffirmation and then reception. A note at the end of this rite states: "Christians from other traditions who have been fully initiated in that tradition may be admitted to communicant membership of the Anglican Church through the rite of Reception into Communicant Membership. The rite that follows may be inserted in Holy Baptism... or in the service of Confirmation.... It may also be used in a service of Holy Communion before the Greeting of Peace. The Canon requires that the bishop be the minister of this rite." Or consider the provisions of WI, Admission of Persons Baptized and Confirmed in Other Communions.

Should we provide in the Additional Directions a text to accompany the giving of a candle at baptism? Differing forms are provided in BAS, SA, Aus, WI, LBW, and BCW.

THE HOLY EUCHARIST

CONSIDER SUBSTITUTING THE WORD "president" for the word "celebrant," as all the baptized are celebrants. ASB, BAS, and WI use the term presiding celebrant; NZ uses the presiding priest.

The rubrics in "Concerning the Celebration" designate that certain parts of the service are properly done by persons in one or another of the four orders of ministers. Note that rubrics within the rite respect the integrity of the order of deacons; in the absence of a real deacon, a priest cannot play deacon, for the deacon's functions are divided among other orders. The deacon's place as reader of the Gospel is performed by the chief celebrant or by an assisting priest; the Prayers of the People are led by a lay person; the table is prepared by the celebrant or an assisting priest; and the celebrant (rather than an assisting priest) does the Dismissal.

At this point, can we not provide one eucharistic rite rather than two? Possibly retain the Prayer for the Whole State of Christ's Church (with slight revision) as an option among the Prayers of the People and retain Eucharistic Prayer II as an option among the Eucharistic Prayers. Print in Additional Directions the Prayer of Humble Access (in sense lines) as an optional use. And as an appendix to the rite (like the appendixes of Offertory Sentences and of Proper Prefaces), along with various Seasonal Blessings from the *Book of Occasional Services*, print the Blessings now in Rite One, for occasional use.

If both Rite One and Rite Two are retained, bring rubrics into conformity so that the basic outline is the same in both rites. Require the Opening Acclamation rather than requiring the Collect for Purity in Rite One. Make Kyrie/Trisagion and the Song of Praise alternatives rather than allowing both in Rite One. Require the Invitation to Communion in Rite One, and require a Dismissal but make a Blessing optional in Rite One. Standardize people's responses, or provide different cues (as for the two forms of the Lord's Prayer) if different people's responses are retained in the two rites (for example, in Rite One: The Lord be with you. **And with thy spirit**; and in Rite Two: God be with you. **And also with you.**).

Among Additional Directions, rubrics from LBW:MDE might be included:

The principal symbol in this service [The Liturgy of the Word] is the Bible or a lectionary which should be of appropriate size and dignity. The service may begin with a procession in which the book may be carried and placed upon the reading desk [pulpit/ambo/lectern].

The focal character of the reading desk is heightened by placing tall, freestanding candlesticks on either side. These may be torches carried in procession.

The Entrance Rite (that is, all that precedes the first Lesson) has been referred to as "our cluttered vestibule." It consists of assorted items that entered the liturgy for various reasons over a period of time. A procession with singing at the entrance of the clergy came into use in the fourth and fifth centuries with the move into large basilicas; including the choir in the procession dates to the late nineteenth century. The Opening Acclamation entered Eastern liturgies in the early medieval period. The Collect for Purity is a remnant of the private preparation of the priest; it came into the public rite in the 1552 revision and the Decalogue entered the rite in the same revision. The Summary of the Law was introduced in eighteenth-century Nonjuror and Scottish use as a complement to the Decalogue. The Kyrie is the remnant of a litany that came into the entrance rite of the Roman liturgy in the sixth century. The Trisagion was a people's refrain in entrance psalms in Eastern liturgies; use of this refrain without its accompanying psalmody eventually came into Gallican rites. The Gloria in excelsis came into regular use at this point in the eucharist in the Roman rite in the eleventh century; various canticles (varying with the seasons), which had been regular parts of the Daily Office, had come into use in Gallican rites at an earlier date. The rubrics of Rite Two allow for enough choices to provide for a fairly straightforward Entrance Rite with a festive or somber nature, or somewhere in between, that is appropriate to various days and seasons. The present rubrics of Rite One still require diverse elements that often frustrate planning a clean entrance rite appropriate for a particular day or occasion.

In the rubric preceding the Gloria in excelsis (324/356), substitute the word *canticle* for the term *Song of Praise*. (I have seen a service sheet that listed "God bless our native land" as the Song of Praise.) But do not altogether rule out the use of a hymn at this point. Among Additional Directions, allow for occasional use of a hymn in place of this canticle, as a hymn is allowed on occasion in place of a canticle in the Daily Offices (142). Insert, at the end of the Additional Directions after the eucharistic rites, a table of canticles appropriate to the various days and seasons comparable to S 355 in *Hymnal 1982* (compare the lists of recommended canticles for use at the eucharist in BAS and SA). Our eucharistic rites should be enriched by use of a wide range of canticles (reminiscent of ancient Gallican usage) rather than the invariable use of Gloria in excelsis, which is still the pattern in many parishes. The Hymnal Committee intentionally did not print Gloria in excelsis among eucharistic music but among the other canticles, and it provided at S 355 in *Hymnal 1982* a chart outlining a richer use of canticles, which seems to have been largely ignored. In addition to providing canticles more appropriate to various days and occasions, this more frequent use of the whole range of canticles would etch these texts into people's memories. If people are exposed to these canticles by singing them in the principal Sunday services, their devotional lives would be enriched as these canticles come to their minds unbidden during the week. Incidentally, when people complain about Morning Prayer being displaced by the eucharist as the principal service, a major complaint is the loss of a range of canticles.

So that it does not interrupt the movement from the Opening Acclamation to the canticle, SA prints the Collect for Purity after the Gloria (or other canticle) for optional use at times when the Kyrie is used rather than a canticle or hymn.

The late medieval period brought forth a plethora of troped Kyries that in the sixteenth century were rejected by the Roman church as well as by the other churches. Yet LBW has a troped Kyrie, and in Aus the confession and Kyrie may be replaced by a Litany of Confession.

> Lord, we have sinned in thought, word and deed:
>   Lord, have mercy.
>   **Lord, have mercy.**
>
> We are truly sorry and we ask you to forgive us:
>   Christ, have mercy.
>   **Christ, have mercy.**
>
> Help us by your Spirit to live in newness of life:
>   Lord, have mercy.
>   **Lord, have mercy.**

Should these and/or other troped Kyries be provided in a revised BCP?

It might be wise to print this rubric from Aus among the Additional Directions:

> In using the collects it will usually help the congregation to pray if a pause is left after the invitation "Let us pray." It will also be helpful if a short break is made before a lengthy final ascription so that the doxology does not overshadow the prayer itself.

Our BCP should, like most of the more recent books, require all three

Lessons and the Psalm on Sundays and Major Holy Days. CW allows "on weekdays which are not Holy Days, the Psalm and either the Old Testament Lesson or the Epistle may be omitted." BAS allows the omission of one Lesson (but not of the Psalm) on days that are not Sundays or major festivals.

It needs to be stated that the Gradual Psalm is an integral part of the rite and not walking music for the lectors.

In previous books, the Gospel was always followed by the Nicene Creed, and that could be followed by announcements, prayers, hymn, and Bidding Prayer or Invocation. Every permission to say or sing anything between "Praise to you, Lord Christ" and the first sentence of the sermon has been quite deliberately deleted, but that needs to be spelled out. The sermon should not be framed off at the beginning from the lections, and it should not be closed off at the end by any ascription but followed by silence for reflection. Or it should lead directly into the Creed or the Prayers of the People. As in BAS, a rubric should follow the sermon: "A silence for reflection may follow."

On baptismal occasions, people confess or renew their faith in the words of the Apostles' Creed, which otherwise is not said on any Sunday or Major Feast. This creed should be said with enough frequency for it to be memorized. We should follow the lead of more recent books (BAS, SA, NZ, Aus, WI, LBW, UMBW, and BCW) in allowing use of the Apostles' Creed in place of the Nicene, possibly on Sundays leading up to baptismal occasions or (like BAS) except on major festivals or in certain seasons, (LBW appoints the Apostles' Creed in Epiphany and the Season after Pentecost.) In BAS, the Nicene Creed is preceded by these words, "Let us confess our faith, as we say." The Apostles' Creed is introduced, "Let us confess the faith of our baptism, as we say." In Aus, the Nicene Creed is introduced, "Let us together affirm the faith of the Church."

The "I believe" form of the Nicene Creed should be removed from Rite One. For ecumenical reasons, in accordance with the resolution of the 1988 Lambeth Conference and in line with other recent Anglican books (BAS, WI), the filioque ("and the Son") should be removed from the Nicene Creed in the phrase "proceeds from The Father and The Son."

It evidently needs to be stated explicitly that using Eucharistic Prayer D does not mean that the Prayers of the People may be omitted.

In forms of the Prayers of the People I, II, and V, intercession is made for classes or special groups rather than for persons: "For the aged and infirm, for the widowed and orphans, and for the sick and the suffering.... For the poor and the oppressed, for the unemployed and the destitute, for prisoners and captives," etc. These should be revised to read "For those who are aged or infirm, those who are widowed or orphaned, and those who are sick or suffering," etc.

In Forms III and VI, in order to keep people from being bookbound and to encourage the participation of children and of those with sight difficulties, move the content of the people's responses up into the leader's part and provide fixed responses for the people. Go back to the 1969 version of Form VI.[2]

After the Prayers of the People, too many celebrants simply fall back on one or another of the prayers about praying that are printed on pages 394-95 rather than choosing, as the prayer book suggests on page 394, a collect appropriate to the season or occasion or expressive of some special need or for the mission of the Church. The last line in the directions should be revised to read, "or, at other times, a general Collect such as the following."

Should a rubric be inserted on pages 330 and 359, prior to the invitation to confession, saying that the Exhortation, pages 316-17, might be read on occasion?

In historic liturgies, sorrow for sinfulness was explicitly expressed in some forms, such as the Kyrie and the Lord's Prayer. But in historic liturgies, the principal expression of confession was in the Eucharistic Prayer, where it took the form of giving thanks to God for having redeemed us from our sins. And in the historic liturgies the absolution was the receiving of the Body and Blood of Christ for the forgiveness of sins. An explicit general confession for the congregation was not a part of eucharistic rites until the continental Reformation, when general confessions came into the rites to take the place of the private confessions that, in the Western church from the twelfth century, had become a normal prerequisite for communion. In "The Liturgy of the Lord's Supper" (1967), the Invitation, General Confession, Comfortable Words, and Absolution (in that sequence) were printed as an appendix to the rite. A rubric directed that this order be used "on the First Sunday in Advent, Ash Wednesday, the First Sunday in Lent, Passion Sunday [the Fifth Sunday in Lent], and the First Sunday after Trinity, and at other times at the direction of the Priest." In the trial rites that followed, this order was printed within the eucharistic rite but never required. The new book might suggest that it is appropriate in Lent and on other occasions. BAS quotes Aidan Kavanagh, "That the Church is reconciled only by verbal confession and absolution is a peculiarly Western absorption that continuously causes sacramental and liturgical problems."[3] BAS has this rubric, "The following prayers [Confession and Absolution] **may** (emphasis added) be used here if the Penitential Rite was not used before the Gathering of the Community, or if penitential intercessions were not used in the Prayers of the People." WI has a striking addition to the confession of sin, "We have not loved our neighbors as ourselves; we have not loved ourselves as we ought. We are truly sorry...." Should the Confession of Sin be printed as an appendix, as it was in the Liturgy of the Lord's Supper (1967)?

On pages 332 and 360 remove the word *may* from the rubric at the bottom of the page, so that it will read, "Then the Ministers and People greet one another in the name of the Lord."

The Preparation of the table often takes on a disproportionate emphasis and consumes an unreasonable amount of time. I once saw it extend to twenty-two minutes; the Eucharistic Prayer consequentially came across as an insignificant appendix. Things are often done sequentially that should have been done simultaneously. The rubrics need to be refined. They might be re-worked to read, "While representatives of the congregation collect the people's offerings of bread and wine and money or other gifts and bring them to the deacon or priest and the table is being prepared for the celebration of the eucharist, a hymn or psalm or anthem may be sung."

As in many recent books, the congregation should be allowed to sit for the Preparation of the Table. In many congregations people now stand throughout the Nicene Creed, the Prayers of the People, the Exchange of the Peace, the Preparation of the Table, the Eucharistic Prayer, the Lord's Prayer, the Breaking of the Bread, the Fraction Anthem, and the Invitation. The people should not have to stand "while the offerings are presented and placed on the Altar," as required by the rubric on pages 333 and 361, but should be directed to assume the standing posture for the Eucharistic Prayer and what follows.

Delete the rubric "Then, facing the Holy Table, the Celebrant proceeds" (pp. 333 and 361). This rubric was not intended to perpetuate an eastward position but to rule out the practice of some "advanced" priests in the late 1960s and early 1970s who stood with their backs to an altar that was still against an east wall as they read the Eucharistic Prayer facing the people.

In the BCP, we have in Eucharistic Prayers B and D forms that are excellent for use in the Advent-Christmas, Epiphany cycle; in Prayers II, A, and C we have forms that are suitable for use in Lent. We need more prayers well adapted for other seasons and occasions and for general use. UMBW, in addition to Eucharistic Prayers printed within the various Services of Word and Table, provides two alternative Thanksgivings for general use and twelve prayers for particular seasons or occasions, and additional prayers for use with particular pastoral or occasional services. BCW provides ten general Eucharistic Prayers plus prayers for particular days or seasons and for particular pastoral or occasional services.

Some of the recent Anglican books, as well as UMBW an BCW, provide a wider range of prayers and recover additional eucharistic imagery that had fallen out of use in liturgical texts or eucharistic iconography in the Western church in the medieval period and was not recovered at the Reformation. Such imagery includes Abraham's hospitality (the most common Eastern eucharistic image), feeding with manna, covenant meals, the wedding at Cana, feeding of the multitudes, eating with outcasts and sinners, and, above all, the resurrection meals and the heavenly banquet. We need prayers that recapture a greater use of such biblical eucharistic imagery. We particularly need one or more prayers for the Easter season that stresses passover imagery, the resurrection meals, and the eschatological banquet (see historic Gallican Eucharistic Prayer). Because of our concordat with the Lutherans, we might also include at least one of the Eucharistic Prayers from LBW:MDE (pp. 221-26). We might also include Eucharistic Prayer I of BAS, which is based on that of the Apostolic Constitutions and which includes such references as "male and female you created us, ...your servants Abraham and Sarah... Moses... He... ate and drank with outcasts and sinners.

Eucharistic Prayer C needs revision. The responses of the congregation in our form are said, in the revised version in BAS, by the celebrant, and the congregation has a fixed response, so that members of the congregation are not bookbound and so that children and those who have sight difficulties are better able to participate. The post-Sanctus portion of this prayer needs to be revised so that it contains (in the order found in the other prayers) an Institution Narrative followed by an anamnesis and oblation and then an epiclesis (note the revised version in BAS). This same sort of revision needs also to be made in the post-Sanctus of Form 1 in "An Order for Celebrating the Holy Eucharist."[4]

Eucharistic Prayer I in the First American *Book of Common Prayer* was certainly a vast improvement over the form of the 1662 English Prayer, for it contained (as the 1662 did not) an anamnesis and an oblation and a sort of epiclesis. But this form lacks elements found in most historic Eucharistic Prayers, such as thanksgiving for creation and incarnation and reference to the Second Coming and, in place of an historic epiclesis beseeching that this bread and wine may be for us the Body and Blood of Christ, it substitutes a petition for worthy reception. For the late eighteenth century, the adoption of this form in place of the 1662 form was a great liturgical and theological step forward. But in Anglicanism for decades we have asserted, in preaching and teaching, that we Anglicans believe in a Real Presence, and this form definitely asserts a receptionistic approach to the Sacrament. It is time to relegate Eucharistic Prayer I to the appendix of historical documents.

All of the more recent Anglican revisions, except Ire and CW, have dropped the requirement of Manual Acts during the reading of the Institution Narrative. Even the restrained use of Manual acts that is required in the Eucharistic Prayers of BCP 79 tends to signify that the Institution Narrative is a moment of consecration, even though it should be obvious to anyone reading the whole of these prayers that the Institution Narrative is in the prayers, not as a formula for consecration, but as a warrant for the celebration of this Sacrament. If these Manual Acts continue to be required, other important moments in the prayer should also be highlighted ceremonially as well, with actions that have substantial historic precedent. The oblation might be marked by raising up or pointing to the elements; the epiclesis, by a sign of the cross or an extension of the celebrant's hands; and the people's Amen might be anticipated by an elevation of the bread and cup.

Remove "kneel or stand/stand or kneel" rubrics following the Sanctus in the Eucharistic Prayer. In Prayer B we give thanks to God for having "made us worthy to stand before you." Rubrics in ASB, BAS, NZ, and Aus assert that the Eucharistic Prayer is a single prayer and that its unity may be obscured by changes of posture in the course of it. Aus then explicitly recommends standing for the whole of the prayer.

The form of the Doxology of Eucharistic Prayer D ("Through Christ, and with Christ and in Christ...") should be substituted for that in the other Eucharistic Prayers.

In the Western church, assisting or visiting presbyters have exercised their priestly function by taking part in the Breaking of the Bread. "It is not generally appreciated that sharing in this action [the Breaking of the Bread] was the distinct concelebratory act in the ancient Roman liturgy."[5] The BCP 79 restores to the Ordination of Priest participation in the Breaking of the Bread as the new priest's first priestly act. We should follow our *Book of Occasional Services* and BAS and UMWB in re-working the rubrics connected with the Breaking of the Bread to set forth more clearly the traditional procedure: "The Celebrant (with assisting priests) breaks the consecrated Bread for distribution." The Additional Directions should probably also contain a note from the *Book of Occasional Services* granting permission for deacons to take part in the Breaking of the Bread in the absence of a sufficient number of priests.

In the Patristic period, the primary images associated with the Breaking of the Bread were Paul's emphasis on one Body, many members, or the Gospel emphases on Christ's being made known in the Breaking of the Bread, and the eucharist as an eschatological feast. The *Book of Occasional Services* and the *Hymnal 1982* have provided additional Fraction Anthems that make use of texts that recover these emphases and of other texts historically associated with the Breaking of the Bread, many of which were used long before either the Agnus Dei or the Christ our Passover were associated with this action, in the late seventh and the mid-sixteenth centuries, respectively. The Roman Catholic scholar Joseph A. Jungmann finds clear evidence only as early as the sixth century of the interpretation of the action of the Breaking of the Bread as a figure of Christ's death on the cross.[6] A wide range of Fraction Anthem texts with a great variety of eucharistic images should be printed in the *Book of Common Prayer* itself *in situ*, or all Fraction Anthems should be printed as an appendix to the rite. Certainly the Agnus Dei and the Christ our Passover should not be given the pride of place. BAS has seasonal Fraction Anthems. All of the newer books give primary place to

Paul's emphasis on the one Body, either in these forms or in a variation of it:

We break this bread to share in the body of Christ
Though we are many, we are one body,
because we all share in the one bread.

In view of the various strata of meanings, it might be suggested that the appropriate ceremonial action at the Breaking of the Bread is not one big breaking of the loaf and showing it divided into two pieces (which suggests a later strata of meanings) but a simple division into the appropriate number of pieces for the assembled congregation.

The direction might be more prominently set forth within the rite, rather than as an Additional Direction, that any additional chalices that are needed should be brought to the altar and filled after the Breaking of the Bread.

Drop the directions "facing the people" from the rubric preceding the Invitation to Communion. Do not print the optional addition to the Invitation within the rite. If it is retained in the book, place it among the Additional Directions (as the contemporary form of Agnus Dei is printed in that place in BCP 79). The eucharist is a multifaceted symbol; this sentence emphasizes one of those facets at the expense of others. This sentence also fosters a Zwinglian interpretation of the rite.

Make it clear that lay ministers may distribute both bread and wine. This allows for a more expeditious administration of communion to the congregation. It also enables the recovery of the ancient practice in which the celebrant, as well as the other communicants, received communion from the hands of another, receiving communion as a gift, rather than as something that they had themselves concocted.[7]

The printing of Amen in italics after the Sentences of Administration certainly implies that the whole sentence should be said to each individual, but it is now obvious that this should have been spelled out.

Print the Blessings of Rite One and the Seasonal Blessings from the *Book of Occasional Services* as an appendix to the eucharistic rite (like Offertory Sentences and Proper Prefaces).

Among the Proper Prefaces, reverse the order of the two for Lent. The second is certainly more appropriate for Ash Wednesday, the first day of Lent, and generally the more appropriate form throughout the season except for the First Sunday in Lent. In WI and LBW this is the only Proper Preface for Lent.

In "Communion under Special Circumstances," print rubrics from BAS: "When a member of the community cannot be present at the community eucharist but wishes to receive communion, it is desirable that members of the community bring the consecrated elements to that person immediately upon completion of the Sunday celebration. This service may be conducted by a priest, or by a deacon or lay person authorized by the diocesan bishop." A model for an (optional) introduction to this rite might be provided, such as that of BAS: "*Brothers and sisters* in Christ, God calls us to faithful service by the proclamation of the word, and sustains us with the sacrament of the body and blood of Christ. Hear now God's word, and receive this holy food from the Lord's table."

Re-work the introductory rubrics of "An Order for Celebrating the Holy Eucharist" along the lines of those of NZ: "This rite requires careful preparation by the presiding priest and participants. It is intended for particular occasions and not for the regular Sunday or weekly celebration of the Eucharist."

Additional Directions

Drop the third paragraph; there is no longer need to perpetuate the older form of Gloria Patri.

Re-work the sixth paragraph so that it conforms to classical Anglican practice and to current Roman norms.[8] All readings (including the Gradual Psalm and the Gospel), as well as the Exsultet, should be read from the one ambo/pulpit/lectern—which represents Christ's presence in his Word as the altar/table represents his presence in the eucharistic Sacrament—and sermons should normally be preached from this place, as well. The permission to read the Gospel from the midst of the congregation should be struck. The Gospel reading is important enough that—like the Lesson, the Gradual, and the Epistle—it should be read from a place where people (including children) can both see and hear. The reading of the Gospel should not be separated from the sermon by a recessional of the Gospel book. Standing to preach in the pulpit from which the Word was read gives the sermon the authority of the Word (and challenges the preacher to bring sermons under the judgment of the Word).

At the top of page 407, print out the Grace (since it has not been defined in the book).

In the directions concerning the Peace, substitute "which follows" for "which may follow." Drop the permission to exchange the Peace at the time of the Invitation.

In the rubric about announcements, page 407, underline or italicize or print in bold print (or all three) the word *Necessary*. Substitute "at the end of the service" for the phrase "before [the blessing and] Dismissal." (I have actually heard in more than one parish, "Go in peace to love and serve the Lord. **Thanks be to God.** Please be seated.") Add after this rubric, from SA, the sentence, "The service should not otherwise be interrupted by the giving of notices." The service should not be interrupted, and people should not be encouraged to be bookbound, by having page numbers or directions concerning posture announced, except in very unusual circumstances when there is no service sheet or hymnboard. Specify that real bread is to be used for the eucharist. That is certainly implied in such rubrics that assisting priests take part in the Breaking of the Bread and that at an ordination all the new priests take part in the Breaking of the Bread. You would think that it would be obvious to anyone that red wine has more sign value in the eucharistic rite than white wine. But maybe the rubric concerning the offertory needs to include qualifications: "Representatives of the congregation bring the people's offerings of *real* bread and *red* wine, and money or other gifts, to the deacon or celebrant."

Insert a rubric from LBW:MDE: "A loaf of leavened or unleavened bread which can be broken and shared is a more adequate sacramental sign than wafer bread." Expand the direction concerning the flagon for additional wine as in BAS, "one chalice on the altar and, if need be, a flagon, decanter, jug, or suitable container of wine from which additional chalices may be filled after the breaking of the bread." Insert after the word *wine*, "not a *cruet* which people associate with oil and vinegar rather than with wine." Or consider the rubric in Aus: "The symbolism of one bread and one cup has great value. It is suggested that one loaf of bread and one chalice of wine only be placed on the table for the Great Thanksgiving. If need be, extra loaves of bread and some suitable jug or other container of wine may also be placed on the table. Other chalices may then be filled from the jug after the Breaking of the Bread."

The direction that only one chalice should be on the altar during the Eucharistic Prayer implies that no ciborium of a type that cannot be distinguished from a chalice by some of the people in the pews should be there beside it. But it seems obvious now that this should have been spelled out. In fact, it should have been spelled out that bread should be in a plate, tray, or basket (that is, a vessel of a type normally associated with bread) rather than in a ciborium.

Add rubrics from BAS: "Care should be taken at the time of the preparation of the gifts to place on the holy table sufficient bread and wine for the communion of the people so that supplementary consecra tion is unnecessary. However, if...." "Communion should be given at each celebration of the eucharist from bread and wine consecrated at the liturgy" (not from the reserved Sacrament). Specify, as the Roman Missal does, that sufficient bread and wine are to be consecrated for the communion of the faithful: "It is most important that the faithful should receive the body of the Lord in hosts consecrated at the same Mass.... Communion is thus a clearer sign of sharing in the sacrifice which is actually taking place."[9]

Remove the text of the Agnus Dei from the Additional Directions and place it in an appendix of Fraction Anthems.

The Additional Directions allow for administration of communion from the reserved Sacrament by a deacon at the conclusion of the Liturgy of the Word. This is not given a name in BCP 79, and it has often been called "deacons mass," a most unfortunate term. NZ provides a descriptive title: "A Service of the Word with Holy Communion." NZ, like current Roman practice, allows a lay person as well as a deacon to preside at this rite: "The bishop may authorize a deacon or a lay person to distribute Holy Communion to a congregation from the Sacrament consecrated elsewhere." NZ includes a prayer for use after the Prayers of the People before the Peace, and an optional prayer that might be used after the Peace before the administration of the Sacrament, neither of which could be mistaken for a Eucharistic Prayer. In this rite, the Lord's Prayer should be introduced in the same manner as at regular celebrations.

Hidden in the Additional Directions that follow the ordination rites (p. 555) is the suggestion that "it is appropriate for the deacons to remove the vessels from the Altar, consume the remaining Elements, and cleanse the vessels in some convenient place." A note to this effect should be inserted among the Additional Directions that follow the eucharistic rite. See BAS: "Any remaining consecrated bread and wine...is consumed at the end of the distribution or immediately after the service. This is appropriately done at the credence table or in the sacristy."

PASTORAL OFFICES

THE RITES AND THE ORDERS INCLUDED IN THIS SECTION are not properly called "offices." This section should be titled "Pastoral Services."

Confirmation

See the section on Baptism and Confirmation (above). Clarify "Concerning the Service." For political reasons, certain sentences were made ambiguous. Drop the permission to use the petitions on pages 305-306. Print here the form in Aus.

The Celebration and Blessing of a Marriage

Define the word *charge* (p. 422) or use it as a subtitle or revise the rubric to read: "A deacon, or an assisting priest, may read the paragraph that begins 'I require and charge you both' and [may] ask for the Declaration of Consent...."

Add to the list of Gospel readings the story of the Wedding at Cana, John 2:1-11, the Gospel most frequently found in ancient marriage rites.

Reword the rubric at the top of page 428: "Then husband and wife shall join their right hands and the Celebrant shall lay *his* right hand directly upon theirs and say...." Compare BCW: "The wife and husband join hands. The pastor may place a hand on their joined hands." The recent innovation of placing a priest's stole on the hands of the couple rather than a laying on of hands is poor symbolism.

The Lord's Prayer should be at the conclusion of the prayers rather than as an introduction to them. The rubric at the bottom of page 428 should be printed immediately before the bidding to the Lord's Prayer. I have seen more than one priest reach the bottom of that page and flush red. At a marriage, the Lord's Prayer should be introduced with the same form of words as at the eucharist.

Add the rubric from LBW:MDE: "Under no circumstances should

the bread and wine be received by the bride and groom to the exclusion of the congregation."

On page 432 expand the rubric to say, "the following is said by the Celebrant," or else print the prayer in sense lines and the Amen in the same typeface as the prayer.

In "An Order for Marriage" (pp. 435-36) require a reading or readings from the Scriptures. In that order also drop the 1928 alternative vows.

A Thanksgiving for the Birth or Adoption of a Child

Consider the inclusion of prayers from BAS: Prayer for the parents (or parent) to say, For the Family, For a Child Born Handicapped. Also look at SA prayers for use giving thanks for the "mother's safety after the death of a child" and at prayers in NZ for various ones to say: parents, single parent, mother, father, adoptive parents, grandparents, and wider family; prayer for use when a child is born handicapped, prayer for natural parents of an adopted child, and prayer for family and home. Look at Aus: For a mother, For a sick mother, For a father and his family, For grandparents and other relatives, For use by adopting parents, For the birth parents of an adopted child, For a child born with special needs, look at WI page 281 (prayers For families) and page 324 (For families and For children born with disabilities).

Consider as an alternative the blessing in NZ.

The Reconciliation of a Penitent

Include a rubric from LBW:MDE: "It is helpful if regular times are established when the pastor is available in a designated place to hear individual confessions."

Restore the sacramental sign of laying on of hands to both forms of "The Reconciliation of a Penitent" by revising the rubric at the top of page 448 to read similarly to its equivalent on page 451: "The priest then lays a hand upon the penitent's head (or extends a hand), saying,...."

Ministration to the Sick

Incorporate materials from "A Public Service of Healing" in the *Book of Occasional Services*: the litany, prayers, and suggested Lessons and psalms.

At the blessing of oil, include a rubric from BAS: "Vessels large enough to be seen clearly by the congregation should be used." Suggest that the oil be consecrated, as the BCP 79 implies (not off at the cathedral or bishop's office but), by the priest of the parish and that it be done at a principal liturgy on an appropriate Sunday. Laying on of Hands or Anointing of the Sick should be celebrated on occasions at a principal service. The Lutheran *Occasional Services* suggests St. Luke's Day and some Sundays that are particularly appropriate because of the appointed Gospel, including the Fourth Sunday in Lent and Propers 6 and 15 in Year A; Propers 8, 10, 18, and 25 in Year B; and the Fifth, Sixth, and Seventh Sundays after the Epiphany and Propers 4, 5, and 23 in Year C.

Expand the rubric prior to the special Postcommunion Prayer: "or the following is said by the Celebrant."

Look at additional prayers for the sick in various new books. See for example, Aus (For the healing of memory) and BCW (For those in a coma or unable to communicate, For an Alzheimer's disease patient, For those giving care to a patient with Alzheimer's disease, For those suffering with AIDS, and For use when a life-support system is withdrawn). Also add prayers for the terminally ill.

Ministration at the Time of Death

In the Litany for the Dying, print the long form of the Lord's Prayer rather than the short form, which often confuses people.

Incorporate a rubric from Aus: "The forms [for anointing or laying on of hands] may be accompanied by the making of the signs of the cross by those present on the forehead of the dying person, recalling our baptism into Christ."

Consider incorporating into the Reception of the Body the LBW form for use when the pall is placed upon the coffin.

The Burial of the Dead

Insert the last rubric in the Ministration at the Time of Death immediately before the last rubric on pages 468 and 490 to give it more prominence: "A member of the congregation bearing the lighted Paschal Candle may lead the procession into the church." Maybe add to the rubric "as at the Easter Vigil and as the Paschal Candle leads the procession to the font at baptisms during Easter Season."

Print as an alternative in Rite Two the prayers of Rite One in contemporary language (see BAS, WI, and LBW). As in other rites, the Lord's Prayer should be the climax of the prayers rather than serving as an introduction to them.

Incorporate a rubric from LBW:MDE: "The congregation must be invited to participate; the bread and wine must not be shared among the bereaved family only."

On pages 482 and 498 expand the rubric to say, "the following is said by the Celebrant," or else print the prayer in sense lines and the Amen in the same typeface as the prayer.

In the Kontakion consider substituting *us* for *me* as in SA.

Under the title "The Committal," insert a rubric from LBW and BCW: "The coffin is lowered into the grave or placed in its resting place." Restore to the rubric that follows the anthem a phrase from the previous BCPs: "While earth is cast upon the coffin **by some standing by** [that is, family, friends, acquaintances], the Celebrant says these words."

Follow the Committal with a rubric, "The grave having been filled *or* the body having been committed to the deep *or* the elements *or* its resting place, the Celebrant says." A recovery of this traditional Anglican practice at the Committal is very therapeutic for family, friends, and acquaintances.

Other new books provide prayers suited to particular situations: After the birth of a stillborn child or the death of a newly born child (ASB, NZ, Aus, UMBW, and BCW); At the burial of a child (BAS, SA, NZ, WI, and UMBW); For the mother of the child, For the father of the child, and When a child dies before being baptized (Aus); After release from suffering, After a sudden death, and After a suicide (NZ and Aus); Prayers for use with children (NZ); Prayers for a married person and Prayers of struggle (Aus).

EPISCOPAL SERVICES
The Ordination Rites
The BCP 79 was set up for a return to the practice of the first half of the Church's history of ordaining persons directly to the order to which they had been called. Note that candidates for ordination to diaconate, priesthood, or episcopate enter the Church as lay persons "without stole, tippet, or other vesture distinctive of ecclesiastical or academic rank or

order." What is implied here may need to be spelled out, for the canons have not yet been brought into conformity with BCP 79.

For all three rites, consider the practice in NZ of preceding the Veni Creator and the period of silent prayer with the title "The Invocation."

In BCP 79 the word *ordination* was substituted for *consecration* in the service in which a person is made a bishop. The word *consecration* had come into use in medieval times when the episcopate was no longer thought of as a distinct order but when a bishop was understood to be a priest who had been set apart (consecrated) to exercise certain functions that other priests could exercise only by deputization. The first Anglican ordinal (1550) spoke again of the episcopate as a distinct order but did not restore the ancient title of the rite. The 1979 book does restore the ancient title *ordination* but has not eliminated, as it should have, all references to the service as a *consecration* (see pp. 510, 511, 513, and 553).

At the ordination of a bishop, the rubric preceding the Gospel should read, as it does at the ordinations of a priest or a deacon, "the Deacon or, if no deacon is present, a priest reads the Gospel."

The rubrics related to the Postcommunion Prayers in the ordination services need to be revised. On pages 522-23 the rubric should read, "one of the bishops says," or else the prayer should be printed in sense lines. On pages 535 and 546-47, the rubric should be expanded to say, "the following is said by the celebrant," or else the prayers should be printed in sense lines and the Amens in the same typeface as the prayers.

In ASB, SA, NZ, and Aus the title of the rite for the ordination of priests is "The Ordination of Priests (also called Presbyters)." In Aus it is explained, "The term 'presbyter' is used in the title for the Ordination of Priests following Richard Hooker, the Episcopal Church of Scotland, *The Alternative Service Book* of the Church of England, and current Roman Catholic and Orthodox usage."

Since taking part in the Breaking of the Bread is the first distinctly priestly action of the newly ordained priest (see p. 554) and the historic sign in the Western church of concelebration at the eucharist, the rubric on page 524 should be expanded to read: "the new priest and other priests stand at the Altar with the bishop, as associates and fellow ministers of the Sacrament, take part in the Breaking of the Bread, and communicate with the bishop."

Include in the Additional Directions a clear statement that deacons and priests are not to be ordained in the same service. This denigrates the diaconate, treating it as if it were simply a stepping stone on the way to priesthood.

In Additional Directions in NZ are two good rubrics: "It is important that a rehearsal be held at the direction of the...bishop" and "Symbols of ministry may be presented to the newly ordained provided they do not obscure the prime significance of what is prescribed in the service."

Compare the "Litany for Ordinations" with the "Litany for Ministry" in Aus (pp. 192-93).

Celebration of a New Ministry
See Stephen M. Kelsey, "Celebrating Baptismal Ministry at the Welcoming of New Ministers" (in *Baptism and Ministry: Liturgical Studies, One*, edi. Ruth A. Meyers [New York: Church Hymnal Corporation, 1994] 19-43). Compare the two liturgies for "Celebration of a New Ministry" in *Occasional Celebrations of the Anglican Church of Canada*.

On page 564, print the Postcommunion Prayer in sense lines or revise the rubric to say, "the Bishop says the following prayer," and print the Amen in italics.

The Dedication and Consecration of a Church
On page 570, allow for a sprinkling of the people after the blessing of the water.

Following classical Anglican norms and the current Roman regulations,[10] provide for the dedication of only one lectern, pulpit/ ambo—from which Lessons (including the Gradual Psalm and the Gospel) and the Exsultet are to be read and sermons normally preached and from which the intercessions may be read.

THE PSALTER
IN THE DIRECTIONS UNDER "Direct recitation" add: "If the selection from the Psalter is being read or if it is being sung without accompaniment, the leader reads or sings to the first asterisk and the congregation joins in at that point." Under "Responsive recitation" print in bold print the words **verse by verse**. Shifting at the asterisk can result in ridiculous and amusing results (see, for example, Ps. 119:3, 18, 36, 106; 120:6; 124:5; 126:6).

Provide a series of Psalter collects similar to those in BAS, Aus, LBW:MDE, and BCW (see Daily Offices above).

PRAYERS AND THANKSGIVINGS
Prayers for the World
Add prayers, blessings, and grace at meals for Interfaith Gatherings (see *Occasional Celebrations of the Anglican Church of Canada*).

Add prayers for Jews and Muslims (see BCW).

Add prayers for civic occasions.

Prayers for the Social Order
Add prayers for the Outcast (see BCW).

Prayers for Family and Personal Life
Add the following prayers:

For the anniversary of one's baptism (the Lutheran *Occasional Services*); For the anniversary of a marriage (the *Book of Occasional Services*, Aus, the Lutheran *Occasional Services*, and BCW); "After loss of pregnancy" (UMBW and BCW); For those suffering abuse (Aus); For those who abuse (Aus); For use at the time of a separation or divorce (Aus, the Lutheran *Occasional Services*, UMBW, and BCW); at the beginning of retirement (UMBW); For the retired (BCW); For the sexually confused (BCW); and For one who has attempted suicide (BCW).

Thanksgiving for the Church
Consider adding Thanksgiving for Heroes and Heroines of the Faith (BCW).

THE LECTIONARY
IN BOTH THE EUCHARISTIC LECTIONARY and the Daily Office lectionary, follow the style of BAS, Aus, and BCW: "Week following Sunday between June 12 and 18 inclusive" rather than "Week of the Sunday closest to June 15." In both lectionaries, number the propers from the First Sunday after the Epiphany rather than from the Sunday closest to May 11 (see BAS and Aus).

Suggest that the week's Daily Office lections and the next Sunday's eucharistic readings be printed in the service sheet to encourage the use of the Daily Offices and preparation for the Sunday and Holy Day eucharists.

The Lectionary for Sundays, Holy Days, and Various Occasions
Consider the current Common Lectionary.

Daily Office Lectionary
Consider rubric in BAS: "The readings of the Daily Office Lectionary may be used at weekday celebrations of the eucharist for which no readings have been provided in the Lectionary, or at Morning Prayer when it is attached to the eucharist as the liturgy of the word; in either case, the Gospel reading, preceded by at least one of the other readings, should be used."

CONCLUSION
MOST OF THESE SUGGESTIONS are attempts to clarify what is implicitly there in BCP 79, in part, by drawing attention to clarifications that have been made in later books. Many of the other suggestions come from the eleven later books listed above. In the revision of BCP 79, these changes should be given serious consideration.

This paper has not dealt with what is possibly the most important issue in prayer book revision at this time, and (except for a few texts in NZ and BCW) this issue has had little effect on the eleven more recent books listed above. This issue is the recovery of a broader range of images for God. Passages of Scripture that include feminine imagery of God should be given greater prominence in the lectionary and in liturgical texts, and forms from earlier periods of church history that made a greater use of feminine imagery should be recovered, for the enrichment of our teaching and of our worship and devotional life.

You Shall Have a Song: Music in Liturgical Renewal

Carol Doran

THE FOLLOWING QUOTATION from the writings of Archbishop William Temple (1881-1944) is posted in the sacristy at Bexley Hall. No one can remember who taped it in that place, but its continuing presence before the eyes of all who approach that room's storage cabinets testifies to the unspoken but corporate agreement that its wisdom continues to be an appropriate word for our own time.

> Worship is the submission of all our nature to God.
> It is the quickening of conscience by God's holiness;
> the nourishment of mind with God's truth;
> the purifying of the imagination by God's beauty;
> the opening of the heart to God's love;
> the surrender of will to God's purpose;
>
> And all of this gathered up in adoration,
> the most selfless emotion of which our nature is capable.
> And therefore the remedy of that self-centeredness
> which is our original sin
> and the source of all actual sin.

Worship is said here to center in the activity of the soul. It emanates from that purity of heart that might rightly prepare the faithful to encounter the Holy One. Its efficacy for the individual involves those spiritual disciplines over which the seeker is thought to have control. The implication is that the quickened conscience, the truth-filled mind, the purified imagination, the undefended heart, and the surrendered will can bring one to adoration of God—that which Temple suggests has power enough to overcome original sin. Music is not mentioned explicitly here, but surely it can be heard singing wherever there is adoration.

LITURGY AND LIFE

MUSING UPON A RECENT EXPERIENCE of liturgy that seemed in its own way to overflow with adoration, I was drawn to wondering what that remarkable Anglican leader of the early twentieth century would have thought about that service. Would he judge it to be authentic worship? How would that experience of liturgy influence his opinion of the liturgical health of the Episcopal Church? And in all this what would he have thought about the music—that art which has contributed so generously to the distinguished reputation of Anglican liturgy?

Twelve people who had come to a conference center for a weekend commission meeting found themselves far from any established congregation on Sunday morning. In the center's recently built chapel we had placed our chairs in the most expansive oval possible in the aisle between the straight rows of seating. We were the Church in that place that day. We were a group of the baptized—some lay, some presbyters, some bishops—who gathered to worship God in the most wonderful way we could manage under the circumstances. We chose to be close to the table rather than to the electronic keyboard in the back of the room, and we could see no purpose in using that appliance's prerecorded hymn accompaniments.

Our Church's usual ritual gestures were almost entirely absent from that prayer book liturgy. We were in such intimate proximity that gestures by the presider intended to be seen by those in a larger space's furthest pew were unnecessary. We sat quietly while presider and readers took their roles in leading our worship; all stood to sing and to pray. We offered one another bread and wine in turn around the circle. There were no special garments or fabric hangings available, so we used none. In fact, had Bishop Temple appeared during the moments of preparation preceding the service, when the group was choosing hymns and assigning leadership roles, we might have been tempted to apologize for what could have appeared to one born in the last century as disrespectful informality in that chapel.

And yet this liturgy was an experience of genuine prayer and community for those who gathered there. The Holy One was deeply desired and truly present in the ritual and the artistry of our making eucharist together. All present contributed to the lengthy reflection following the reading of the Gospel. Because music was a language well known to all gathered there that day, our sung prayer was offered confidently and passionately. For many in the group, the music probably was the entrance into the deepest praise and delight in God that morning. Texts and music sung were simple but had been chosen specifically with the occasion, the tradition, the worshippers, and the available musical and printed resources in mind.

The participation had been so full-bodied and so natural that, after it ended, I felt gratitude and joy, rather than an inclination to reflect upon what had happened during that liturgy. Several hours later, one among us took the opportunity to describe to others, who by then had joined us, the wonder he had felt during that time of worship. Only then did I realize how rare and wonderful the experience had been. Since that moment, involuntary and persistent reflection upon what happened in the midst of our *ad hoc* circle that day has reminded me of the ways in which we make assumptions about possibilities for liturgy that are wonderfully harmonized with the belief system of the worshippers.

Professor Leonel L. Mitchell reminds us that "the church's understanding of itself and its worship is constantly growing and unfolding."[1] Surely this also is true of the many individuals who make up the Church. Our conversations with others and our observations of their behavior, our encounter with scripture and our prayer, our reading and our evaluation of media presentations all push and pull us to new vistas from which we must re-harmonize our life situations and our understanding of God. Having refreshed our internal understandings, then, and even having gradually changed our patterns of personal prayer to reflect new awareness, we are faced with the most complex challenge of all: re-negotiating with the others with whom we pray in community. Perhaps they will be open to new insights; perhaps at the present time they will not. How is integrity of prayer to be measured?

The Catechism reminds us that "prayer is responding to God, by thought and by deeds, with or without words."[2] So it is our task and the task of prayer book and hymnal compilers and editors to express those developing understandings in our liturgies—with or without words. The phrase *lex orandi, lex credendi* (rule of prayer, rule of belief) has been a valued principle of liturgical integrity for centuries.[3] But assuring its ongoing validity requires never failing vigilance. Liturgy and life are one.

But people who care about liturgy and music often are pummeled by accusations that we are devoted to matters with little meaning in the "real world," where "styles" of life and "star" status appear to have high value. We cannot dismiss these criticisms as irrelevant to a discussion of liturgical renewal. Liturgists and musicians live in that same world and know that the devastation faced by homeless people, for example, is neither easily comprehended nor to be compared with problems of rubrical obsolescence.

But if our prayer is to respond to God with honesty, it must be reformed constantly but almost imperceptibly—the way children and plants grow. Only when we forget to notice what has happened or when we resist acknowledging the changes before us are we faced inevitably with accumulated grief. Then our lives and our schedules are devastated for the weeks, months, or years that are required for education, healing, and reconciliation until liturgy becomes the people's genuine prayer once more. Liturgy and life are one.   Our prayer inspires our service; our service informs our prayer. Archbishop Temple's definition of worship understands this.

EARLY ATTITUDES TOWARD MUSIC AND THE LITURGY

THE IMPLICATIONS FOR MUSIC'S ROLE in such expanded liturgical understanding are significant. Archbishop Temple (in the quote above) describes adoration, for example, as emotion. But he does not suggest how emotion in corporate worship might look or sound. Many, in fact, have intentionally avoided thinking about such things, let alone discussing them with others. The fourth-century bishop Augustine of Hippo was suspicious of emotions in corporate worship. Here he is expressing his ambivalence about music's place in liturgy:

> The pleasures of the ear did indeed draw me and hold me more tenaciously, but You have set me free. Yet still, when I hear those airs, in which Your words breathe life, sung with sweet and measured voice, I do, I admit, find a certain satisfaction in them, yet not such as to grip me too close, for I can depart when I will. Yet in that they are received into me along with the truths which give them life, such airs seek in my heart a place of no small honor, and I find it hard to know what is their due place.

At times, indeed, it seems to me that I am paying them greater honor than is their due—when, for example I feel that by those holy words my mind is kindled more religiously and fervently to a flame of piety because I hear them sung than if they were not sung; and I observe that all the varying emotions of my spirit have modes proper to them in voice and song whereby, by some secret affinity, they are made more alive.

It is not good that the mind should be enervated by this bodily pleasure. But it often ensnares me in that the bodily sense does not accompany the reason as following after it in proper order, but, having been admitted to aid the reason, strives to run before and take the lead. In this matter I sin unawares, and then grow aware.[4]

Augustine acknowledges music's ability to make texts "more alive." In fact, at a later point in this section, he remembers "the tears I shed, moved by the songs of the Church in the early days of my new faith." But in the final analysis, he appears to fear music, implying that it possesses power stronger than his ability to withstand it.

Thus I fluctuate between the peril of indulgence and the profit I have found: and on the whole I am inclined—though I am not propounding any irrevocable opinion—to approve the custom of singing in church, that by the pleasure of the ear the weaker minds may be roused to a feeling of devotion.

Yet whenever it happens that I am more moved by the singing than by the thing that is sung, I admit that I have grievously sinned and then I should wish rather not to have heard the singing.[5]

Augustine suggests that the presence of music in worship might be justified as a means of encouraging devotion in "weaker minds" and then confesses regret that even his presumably stronger mind had "grievously sinned" by being moved by the singing. He wrestles with the possibility of recommending the elimination of music with all its acknowledged benefits in order to safeguard against future temptations. Clearly, he believes that having pleasure in music, even though it be unsolicited and unexpected, is sin. His solution to this danger is to eliminate the temptation altogether by eliminating music itself from worship.

The earliest Christians also opposed the use of music—particularly instrumental music—but for a different reason. Because music was so intimately associated with pagan rituals of sacrifice, Clement of Alexandria (ca. 150 - ca. 215) forbade the use of "these instruments at our temperate banquet."[6] Their opposition to flutes, tambourines, and stringed instruments also was motivated by the ability of pagan musicians to entice many new converts back to their former practices.

But early Christian disdain for musical instruments was tempered by well-known Jewish traditions that included their use. Because of their former lives as Jews, many early converts knew well the ordinances in the Hebrew bible about musical practices that had been commanded by God through the prophets.[7] And the psalms themselves, as well as their superscriptions,[8] frequently direct the faithful to praise God with ram's-horn, lyre, harp, timbrel, strings, pipe, cymbals, and other instruments.[9]

In addition to their fear of music's power to persuade and their disdain for the circles in which it moved, early Christians had a primary theological argument against instrumental music. They believed that the complexity and multiplicity of sounds created by musical instruments playing together was antithetical to the "primitive Christian idea of the divine unity and the communion of souls."

> We want to strive so that we, the many, may be brought together into one love, according to the union of the essential unity. As we do good may we similarly pursue unity.... The union of many, which the divine harmony has called forth out of a medley of sounds and division, becomes one symphony, following the one leader of the choir and teacher, the Word, resting in that same truth and crying out: "Abba, Father."[10]

But attempts by community leaders to restrain music go back even further than the first century. Consider, for example, Plato's well-known disdain for the excesses of poetry and music. This fourth century (B.C.E.) Greek philosopher argued quite logically that certain harmonies, rhythms, and modes were "unsuitable to our State."[11]

But he also argued that "wives and children are to be in common"[12] and that "mean employments and manual arts [are] a reproach."[13] His arguments are logical, but they often are unable to accommodate important exceptions. Either this or that is understood to be true, but there is no room for what Urban Holmes (following Victor Turner and Arnold van Gennep)[14] has called the *liminal*,[15] that experience of being on the boundary. Symbol power in art, which is one of its fundamental strengths, emanates directly from its ability to lead the viewer, listener, or participant out of a certain category into other possibilities or associations. Plato and others did not feel comfortable trusting people with unlimited possibilities.

In a number of ways, Plato's convictions about the importance of reason in society were very much like Augustine's. Reason is given first place and all other considerations are subservient—"in proper order." Augustine, as quoted above, acknowledges the benefits of music by noting its ability to kindle his mind "more religiously and fervently to a flame of piety."

Music's role in liturgical renewal today inevitably will be influenced by the thinking and writing of many early and influential church leaders who find the words of Plato and Augustine persuasive. Rather than use these historic documents to suggest genetic imperfections associated with musical talent, however, we might consider those writings in light of sociological, psychological, and ecclesiastical developments that have brought us much insight and knowledge since Plato's time.

Anthropology, after all, emerged as an independent science only in the late eighteenth century. The disciplines of congregational studies, pastoral music, and ritual music have enlarged our vocabulary and our perspective on liturgical music. Today we are able to discuss the first centuries of the Christian experience and every century since in the light of significant new scholarship and historical sources, so it is important to blend these new perspectives into the liturgical developments of a new day.

Bringing certain lurking fears into the light of open discussion will contribute to better understanding but will not guarantee their healing. How can we neutralize the effect of well-meaning religious education that has left us wondering if joy in church involves sin? But a closer look at the documents that have denigrated music and musicians and an inquiry into the nature of emerging models of music leadership in Christian congregations will, at the very least, enlarge the discussion of music's potential to enhance worship. In the same way that we re-examine liturgical history for clues about what brought efficacy to people's prayer, let us here consult church history for previously hidden models for the liturgical role of the noble art of music.

MUSIC IN FORMATION OF FAITH

PLATO, LIKE HIS PHILOSOPHICAL kinsman Augustine, is not completely opposed to music; but he, like Augustine, obviously is ambivalent about it. Much of Plato's writing in *The Republic* acknowledges music's ability to express moods; he insists that melody, rhythm, and words should be subject to the laws of the state because of their power to influence the citizenry. And although he recommends the banishing of *certain* musical instruments[16] and *certain* modes of music[17] because of their ability to draw people into particular moods and actions, Plato claims music to be fully one-half of the states' "heroes'" education: "And what shall be their education?

Can we find a better than the traditional sort?—and this has two divisions, gymnastic for the body, and music for the soul."[18]

Plato bravely encounters the question that challenged his community and ours as well: How does art affect human beings? How is the wonder of art to be brought into appropriate service of the people? What is the potential of art to lead the community? His ethical concerns are related to our spiritual ones:

[Socrates] Let our artists... be those who are gifted to discern the true nature of the beautiful and graceful; then will our youth dwell in a land of health, amid fair sights and sounds, and receive the good in everything; and beauty, the effluence of fair works, shall flow into the eye and ear, like a health-giving breeze from a purer region, and insensibly draw the soul from earliest years into likeness and sympathy with the beauty of reason.

There can be no nobler training than that, he replied.

And therefore, I said, Glaucon, musical training is a more potent instrument than any other, because rhythm and harmony find their way into the inward places of the soul, on which they mightily fasten, imparting grace, and making the soul of him who is rightly educated graceful, or of him who is ill-educated ungraceful; and also because he who has received this true education of the inner being will most shrewdly perceive omissions or faults in art and nature, and with a true taste, while he praises and rejoices over and receives into his soul the good, and becomes noble and good, he will justly blame and hate the bad, now in the days of his youth, even before he is able to know the reason why; and when reason comes he will recognize and salute the friend with whom his education has made him long familiar.[19]

The question in the center of the discussion that precedes this excerpt is whether artists should be banned because of their potential to corrupt "the taste of citizens." Plato, using Socrates' voice in this writing, recommends instead that, when artists are gifted "to discern the true nature of the beautiful and graceful," then the youth will "dwell in a land of health." He testifies to the potency of music to form people and speaks of its ability to make their souls graceful and their minds perceptive and able to judge both good and bad.

These ancient wise words will be good counsel to us as we consider music appropriate for liturgy and for the ongoing life of the Church. Both mature and young Christians are influenced by the sounds heard, not only in the larger world in which they live, but in the church's nave, during youth group meetings, and at times of Bible study and other Christian education. Is it music freshly made or is it warmed over, having been recorded at another time and place for another occasion or for commercial purposes? Does it make you hold your ears or grit your teeth? Does it bore you into drowsiness?

Music for the life of the Church must be vitally alive, prepared for a specific occasion, and the best we ourselves can provide. The genuine musical testimony of a member of our own community has a unique capacity to express faith and to model liturgical excellence. Music made at the moment of its offering is aware of and responds to the community.

And the community, in listening to it, makes that music its own prayer.

MUSIC SINGS A SPLENDID VARIETY OF SONGS

NEITHER THE NATURE OF MUSIC nor human nature has changed in drastic ways since Plato's time. We do not have the same *names* for "modes," melodies, or musical textures that are able to draw us into certain moods. Some of these responses are related to memory, but according to the work of the neurophysiologist Manfred Clynes and others, the precise physiologic forms characteristic of emotion are communicated (across cultural boundaries) nowhere more effectively than in the arts.[20] These studies show that one culture's joyful music can be recognized as "crucially similar" in other cultures (not always with certainty, but with exceedingly high probability").

Liturgical planning that goes beyond planning the words to be used in the rite should consider the styles and moods of music. One congregation's favorite *Sanctus* is another congregation's frustrating experience. Even the many compositions in the *Hymnal 1982* written for the "Holy, holy, holy Lord" text sing in different moods. Some reflect the dignity and holiness that can surround that moment in the eucharistic prayer. The regular, rousing beats of others encourage us to see ourselves as people of God singing our praise with vigor and determination.

Our present prayer book has few rubrical directions for specific texts to be sung during the liturgies: the hymns "Veni Creator Spiritus" or "Veni Sancte Spiritus" at ordinations and "All glory, laud, and honor" on Palm Sunday are two such directions. Adding more seems ill advised. It would be better to publish a companion to this volume that would suggest musical options according to a number of categories. Marion Hatchett's fine *Hymnal Studies Five: A Liturgical Index to The Hymnal 1982* could form its foundation.[21] Further additions of hymns for each liturgical occasion could be categorized as "easily accessible," "of medium difficulty," or "musically challenging." Such a volume could also contain brief essays about musical choices for various seasons and about the general characteristics of music suitable for liturgy's many "moods" of prayer. These would help musicians who are working on their own to acquire liturgical skills and would assist ordained leaders whose seminary education did not include musical considerations for liturgy.

The Catechism in the *Book of Common Prayer 1979* (p. 856) mentions seven principal kinds of prayer. We could understand these to be principal moods or modes of private as well as corporate prayer; they also remind us of the varieties of music. These types are adoration, praise, thanksgiving, penitence, oblation, intercession, and petition. Not only do these specific types of prayer seem suited to certain appropriate musical textures, melodies, and harmonies, but in several cases, they also have forms that seem to contribute strongly to their effectiveness.

Consider the difference between the types at either end of that list. Petition is described in the Catechism (BCP, p. 857) as the prayer in which we present our own needs (as contrasted with intercession, in which we bring before God the needs of others) "that God's will may be done." When such prayers are sung, the solemnity with which we approach God would suggest moods of simplicity and quietness. Their task is to express needs that may have developed recently, and this kind of prayer is seldom formed into poetry ahead of time. So the musical setting is often a simple tone that ends with a phrase such as "Lord in your mercy" as cue to a response such as "Hear our prayer." Use of a simple monotone for each petition also would make possible, and perhaps invite, spontaneously added petitions by the assembly. An example of such a tone with a simple ending is given in the *Hymnal 1982* (H 82) at S108.22

Adoration, by contrast, is thought to be the most generous kind of praise, in which we give ourselves without reservation to the adoring. The Catechism (BCP, p. 857) says, "Adoration is the lifting up of the heart and mind to God, asking nothing but to enjoy God's presence." To reflect that, music could use broad melodies and rich harmonies. "Let all mortal flesh keep silence" (H 82, p. 324) immediately suggests itself for use at a moment of adoring prayer. Some congregations find themselves in that mood during communion; others have developed a practice of singing more than one hymn of praise at the beginning of the eucharistic liturgy until the mood becomes one of deep adoration.

The tempo at which this (or any hymn or song) is sung should depend on the acoustics of the place of worship as well as on the mood in which the people are offering their sung prayer. Could there be a beginning of moderate tempo and middle-range loudness? Could the singing grow louder and the tempo broaden as each stanza unfolds? Could the final phrase of the last stanza conclude with a major chord on the note

D, to express particular exhilaration, rather than on the customary minor one? Yes! All these lively changes could be encouraged by the ministry of the congregation's music leader.

THE ROLE OF THE MUSICIAN

ONCE CHOSEN, MUSICAL SELECTIONS MAY BE TRANSFORMED (positively or negatively) by the process of interpretation. Musical notation on the page is the merest outline of the wonder of the music. The sounds of congregational song, choir presentation, or instrumental music that are formed in the imagination of the music-makers are stimulated initially by the written symbols, but the souls, minds, and bodies of the singers and instrumentalists shape the sounds that eventually are produced. Whether the music in our churches begins with notes on the printed page or with a memory or a spontaneous prayer, the one who leads and/or accompanies the music contributes substantially to the congregation's experience of the Holy.

Who are these leaders? Where do they come from? How are they formed for leadership? How do they understand their role and responsibility for leading the congregation's worship? How do the ordained leaders with whom they are colleagues understand their own and the musician's role in the people's sung prayer?

Our present prayer book is largely silent regarding the agents who carry out the rubrical directions about music in liturgy. There are seven instances in which singing is assigned to clergy (bishops, priests, or deacons)[23] and three in which the congregation "then sings . . ."[24] But fully 117 rubrical entries direct simply that music of a specific type (psalm, hymn, anthem, proper preface, antiphon, Gloria Patri, canticle, litany, etc.) "is" or "may be" sung.[25] The one responsible for collaborating with the ordained leader to choose the music, lead the congregation, or rehearse the choir or the cantor is neither named by title nor referred to in any way.

Future prayer books would do well to acknowledge in writing the presence and role of the congregation's musical leader. The quality of future music leadership in our church will be affected by the dignity of such naming. Adding the simple words *The Musician* before "shall sing" or "shall lead the people in singing" would bring out of the realm of the invisible those whose service is needed by the churches now more than ever. Many congregations are exploring the use of titles other than "organist/choirmaster" in Episcopal churches. Designations such as "pastoral musician" or "director of music ministries" have helped congregations to become aware of the newly expanded nature of the musician's role. They have also provided an accurate description of the musician's work.

Anthropologist of religion Mircea Eliade writes of the importance in many cultures of giving a new name to one who has participated in a life-changing experience. He writes, "Now for all pre-modern societies the individual's name is equivalent to his true existence, to his existence as a spiritual being."[26] The Episcopal Church would benefit by recognizing the positive transformation in musical leadership presently under way. Its name must be spoken and written; its role in building up the Church must be celebrated.

The well-recognized current crisis in music in our churches is related to this matter. How can we persuade capable musicians to take their appropriate part in church leadership? We can include liturgical catechesis for all the baptized that promotes an understanding of music ministry as a response to gifts given before birth. Most musicians of faith find great satisfaction in working with others to make music in the church, but few enjoy offering their best efforts in an environment where they feel invisible. A respectful title and the professional treatment accompanying it would transform a "church job" into "lay ministry." Such transformations can have greater value than a large salary for musicians working in churches with restricted funds.

Recognizing the ministry of the musician and bestowing an appropriate name on the minister is central to restoring respect to this office. Episcopalians arranging chairs for an informal service of morning prayer automatically ask one another, "Who will lead?" (meaning, "Who will lead our spoken prayers?"). But seldom do we ask, "Who will lead our sung prayers?" In most of our communities, the only realistic answer is "No one here can do that."

There is no reason to believe that the musical gene pool within the Anglican communion has radically changed since the golden age of cathedral music. People in our churches, large and small, have musical talent and an interest in using it. To engage them as leaders, we must appeal to them as people of faith who can offer their musical talents as their reasonable service.

The Leadership Program for Musicians Serving Small Congregations, now operating in many dioceses, has been organized specifically for this purpose. Under the sponsorship of the Standing Commission on Church Music and the Virginia Seminary, this program offers musicians and clergy opportunities to develop their abilities to lead and accompany music as well as to explore the essentials of good liturgy. Participants are formed professionally, musically, and spiritually. This vision for revitalized music leadership is being reclaimed in our day. We are acknowledging what human beings have always known intuitively—that melody, rhythm, repetition, and other characteristics of music have enabled people to approach the Holy.[27] Isn't it reasonable that a Church like ours would give attention and resources to encourage the development of people who can help us worship God through music?

Lawrence Hoffman has written, "liturgy—like linguistics—is not a literary matter in the first place... prayers are not readings, and prayer books are not literary specimens."[28] Anglicans have a fabulous tradition of sonic spirituality. Episcopalians have a splendid hymnal. Renewed musical leaders enable us to do more than just stay together as we sing. Nothing less than transformation of ourselves and our worship is envisioned here.

Let us return for one last time to the early Church's dilemma about music's association with pagan sacrifice rituals. Johannes Quasten writes,

> The Apostolic Age bears witness to the joyful character of early Christianity, particularly as it was expressed in singing. In Ephesians 5:19 Paul calls upon Christians to "address one another with psalms, hymns and spiritual songs, singing and making melody to the Lord in your heart." Colossians 3:16 also refers to singing "psalms and hymns and spiritual songs with thankfulness in your hearts to God."

> These words clearly express the Apostle's conviction that singing is a fitting way to honor God.... In both passages [however] he adds what seems to be a warning against a purely aesthetic pleasure in singing: such singing must take place "in your heart." This articulates well the primitive Christian posi-

tion on liturgical singing. Only insofar as singing is the expression of an inner disposition of devotion does it have any meaning.[29]

Paul and others certainly were aware that some of the baptized and some prominent church leaders had strong objections to music. Here the minority voice (if Paul could be called such) acknowledges the gift of music to enable the congregation's praise and prayer. In light of its potential, Paul and others chose not to make idols of the "exaggerated spiritualistic tendency which regarded music as an obstacle to [worship] and portrayed the renunciation of music in liturgy as the higher ideal."[30] Rather, they raised up the power of music as their own sacrifice.

A poem from the second century contrasts the singing of Christians with pagan sacrifice:

> We may not approach the interior of the temple or pour out libations to pictures of the gods or offer worship with vows,... But, rejoicing in holy speech, with a happy heart, with the rich gift of love and generous hands, with psalms and hymns worthy of our God, we are encouraged to sing your praise, O eternal and unerring One.[31]

Liturgical integrity requires eternal vigilance. It calls us to do justice, to seek a deeper knowledge of God, and to respond to God with all that we are and all that we have. Music, with its vast ability to stimulate and express the spiritual, should be an autonomous and significant theological resource.[32] But too often it has instead been assigned the task of mere illustration. Sometimes this happens out of fear that music will exceed customary restraints. Its inherent character may draw all of our physical bodies into praising, until we may be even tempted to dance and to embrace other Christians. To some, this may seem irreconcilable with the norms of worship they were taught as children.

SUMMARY

THIS ESSAY HAS REVIEWED some arguments against the creative use of music in churches. Many of these arguments originated in the earliest centuries of our Church. Even today some parishioners consider such ideas as "good enough for the early Church, so good enough for me." But our discussion of other ideas from the same period has demonstrated that the early Church valued music a great deal. This indicates that the Church will find in music a treasure not yet fully explored.

Liturgical renewal that more fully utilizes the strength of music will require the support of church resources. Everyone can sing, but most leaders of singing need preparation for their ministry. We need, first of all, to start assuming this can be done. Successful enterprise begins with a dream and then is carried out through faith and determination. Churches that have stopped lamenting the condition of the old organ and established an organ fund are aware of the transforming power of a hope made tangible in a plan. Through the Leadership Program for Musicians Serving Small Congregations,[33] through seminary education for musicians,[34] and through mentoring relationships with knowledge-able clergy and pastoral musicians, the Episcopal Church is capable of including the wonder of music in the continuing renewal of its prayer and praise.

The twelve gathered in the conference center chapel were living into that dream through the oneness of their prayers and their music. I trust that Archbishop Temple would recognize our unassuming liturgy as having been planned with his vision in mind. In the same way, Isaiah's vision can so empower liturgy in churches that our joy in our prayer will supercede any need to discuss it.

> You shall have a song
> as in the night when a holy festival is kept;
> and gladness of heart,
> as when one sets out to the sound of the flute
> to go to the mountain of the Lord,
> to the Rock of Israel.[35]

Reflections on Canon Law and Liturgical Revision: Fostering a *Novus Habitus Mentis* in the Episcopal Church

Leigh Axton Williams

[O]f law there can be no less acknowledged, than that her seat is the bosom of God, her voice the harmony of the world: all things in heaven and earth do her homage, the very least as feeling her care, and the greatest as not exempted from her power, both Angels and men and creatures of what condition soever, though each in different sort and manner, yet all with uniform consent, admiring her as the mother of their peace and joy.[1]

Richard Hooker published these words at the close of the sixteenth century to an embattled English church. We read them, four centuries later, as a Church no less conflicted. Our skirmishes may seem more diffused, our adversaries more multifarious than those against whom Hooker defended the role of law in the life of the Church in England. However, Hooker's Puritan opponents were people of Christian faith; we live in a world where the Christian gospel is viewed by many as nothing more than one reasonable alternative among a host of options proffered to shrewd consumers of matters "spiritual."

Few today would share Hooker's view of law as residing in "the bosom of God," with a voice that is "the harmony of the world" and to whom "all things in heaven and earth" pay homage and admire as "the mother of their peace and joy." Instead, many picture law today, not as an instrument of justice for all people, but simply as a device to be manipulated for personal gain or protection by anyone with sufficient influence and financial resources to do so. Importing this critical secular attitude into the Church has tended to exacerbate a view of canon law as divorced from the living community of faith rather than canon law as an integral part of our common life, a means by which we govern ourselves and our relationships with other people. We must—and can—restore a respect for canon law in the life of the Episcopal Church.

My purpose in this essay is to propose a new agenda for us in our understanding and use of canon law in the Anglican tradition. Law in its secular context is conceived as providing the framework for a community's common life. Why does the Church today seem to have become so reluctant to embrace a similar understanding of the role of canon law? We rarely examine canon law in its broader historical and theological context. As others have observed,where canon law is studied at all it is most frequently scrutinized from the perspective of specific, contemporary canons and how one must either obey or avoid them.[2] To suggest that the Episcopal Church should reclaim a more intentional and scholarly approach to the study of canon law, as a fundamentally *theological* enterprise, exploring the development of canon law and the canon law tradition in the Christian Church (and in American Anglicanism in particular), is not to advocate a return to the kind of troglodytic antiquarianism that characterized most views of canon law and canonists in recent years.[3] Instead, it summons us to restore a serious and intentional study of and reflection on the relationship between God and all of humanity and on our definition of our human relationships, both ecclesial and individual. The shift away from such a historical and theological understanding of canon law has occurred gradually since the early decades of this century.[4] The Episcopal Church historically viewed canon law as playing an essential part in these kinds of inquiries, and our modern unwillingness to engage in such intentional efforts is, I suggest, evidence of a persistent and encroaching anti-intellectualism that has not served us well. As we prepare to cross the threshold of the third millennium, it is time to explore new and more effective paths, aided by a *novus habitus mentis*.

The expression *novus habitus mentis*, "new habit of mind," was a favorite of Paul VI, who used it to define the process of discovery by which the law's true purposes are discerned in the context of the believing community. It can never be merely the adoption of some theological agenda nor does it simply re-formulate, re-interpret, or re-implement old rules in a new context. A new attitude of mind renews the mind itself, the means by which human reason considers propositions, not the propositions the mind contemplates. Jesuit canonist and theologian Ladislas Örsy suggests that such an attitude implies a new method of operation, reflecting that an attitude of mind cannot be anything else than a permanent disposition of the human spirit, the spirit that by its very nature is both contemplative and active. It is contemplative because it has the capacity to seek the truth, to recognize it, and to surrender to its imperative. It is active because it has the capacity to reach out for values, to make responsible decisions and to transform the world through constructive actions. It follows that a new attitude of mind must consist in an internal capacity to operate in new ways; that is, in an improved method of searching for the truth and in an increased determination to reach out for values not noticed before.[5]

For Örsy, acquiring a new attitude of mind demands that people and institutions "ascend to new heights and from there take a fresh look at the world that was so familiar to them."[6] Because Paul VI believed that the Roman Catholic Church was empowered by such a new attitude of mind by the Second Vatican Council, Örsy reflects on the Council's achievements and the method that produced them. He argues that Vatican II effected a "felicitous synthesis of old and new."[7] In so doing, the Roman church began to move from an understanding of itself as *imperium* to a recognition of Church as *communio*. It began to change from an attitude of confessional conflict to one of increasing ecumenical understanding, from a posture of defensive isolation to an appreciation of (but not an absorption by) secular values, and from a philosophy capable of thinking only in static categories to one in which it became possible to think developmentally.[8]

Although we in the Anglican communion are not bound by the precepts of Vatican II, we have been affected, in many significant ways, by the spirit of *aggiornamento* engendered by the Council. Örsy's philosophical and theological process, as reflected in the life of the Roman Catholic Church since Vatican II, has also been, and remains, an essential part of our Anglican ethos. We, too, are examining the shift from a "horizon of power" to a "horizon of service."[9] We, too, have become more receptive to ecumenical overtures and less defensively isolated, and we have become increasingly open to the development of doctrine in new ways. All of these things, for Örsy, evidence this ecclesial realization of a new attitude of mind that, aided by the Church's willingness to inculcate new knowledge, permits us to assume a new and fresh perspective and to pose, address, and answer new questions.[10] The result is a Church that enters "a new field of vision; that is, into a new horizon."[11]

Örsy suggests that the historical and theological evolution of canon law and its traditions has been such a process of changing horizons. The Church has been challenged by new knowledge about humanity, new understandings of God, and new perspectives on human community and the role of law in it. In response, canon law, which is called to be the instrument of Church's justice, increasingly reflects a balance between the practical needs of the community of faith and the duty of service to the world. Canon law has always begun by asking about God and, Örsy cautions, has been shaped by the Church's image of God. This image has changed, and canon law changed with it. The horizon, the field of vision, of canon law always includes the theological understanding of God and asks how law is intended to please God. We answer that question according to our image and understanding of God. In this fractious and fragmented world, we face the same danger our predecessors did: Do we make God over into our image and to suit our agendas? It is easy and tempting to critique the past, but Örsy reminds us that "we should not think that all those who, at various times in our past history, imposed on the community and administered seemingly cruel or senseless laws were necessarily evil or corrupt people. Many of them were convinced that they were doing a service to God; they thought God was the type of person who thought in the same way as they did." Could not the Church apply these words to those who executed William Laud and Thomas Cranmer, John Hus and William Sawtrey, Bernard Mizeki, James Hannington, and Maximillian Kolbe?

Örsy recognizes the innate attractiveness of his theory because of its intuitive appeal to what we sense about human knowledge and experience. To Örsy, however, our inability to resolve disputes rests in a conflict of horizons (and not simply because we fail to explain our positions satisfactorily to those with whom we disagree). This raises a further complication. If we truly desire a "concordance of discordant horizons," both personal and ecclesial horizons must expand.[12] This demands a reassessment of our identity and perhaps change. It can be deeply threatening, particularly when an individual or an institution is uprooted before sufficient time has passed to permit the new perspective to attach itself, to be assimilated on the deepest level, and to grow.

Our experiences with liturgical revision illustrate this process of uprooting, re-assessment, and assimilation and the pain, confusion, and resistance that can result.[13] To address the process, Örsy proposes a specific method of interpretation from the Roman Catholic tradition.[14] As we contemplate further such renewal and revision in the Episcopal Church, we might consider whether Örsy's method can be applied usefully in an Anglican context and how it might aid us in posing proper questions, assimilating new knowledge, and adjusting our horizons as individuals and as a worshiping community.

I want to return to a more basic question: How does the effort to re-claim a theological foundation for canon law, enabled by an adoption of a *novus habitus mentis* and the concomitant expansion of both individual and ecclesial horizons, reveal itself in the context of liturgical revision generally? How has the relationship between liturgical revision and canon law been defined in the Episcopal Church? All liturgy expresses, in part, our human desire to experience the Divine presence, and liturgical law intends to preserve this authentic expression of the Church's self-revelation (rather than solely to govern the activities of our worship) then examining liturgical rites according to a disciplined process of inquiry should display to us more clearly the mystery of Christ that imbues liturgical rite and the spirit, the expression, of the holy things they signify. This should draw us into deeper and more intimate contact with the living God from whom all law draws its authority.[15]

Authority to create and revise worship in the Episcopal Church is governed by the provisions of the *Book of Common Prayer* and the *Constitution and Canons* of the church. The Preface of the first *Book of Common Prayer*, ratified in 1789, affirms plainly both the right to establish an American liturgical use independent of the Church of England and a profound desire to remain in continuity with Anglican tradition.[16] Article 8 of the original *Constitution of the Episcopal Church*, adopted in 1789, provided for a *Book of Common Prayer* to be used in the American church.[17] The *Constitution*, as amended, also provides for an approved process of prayer book alteration and, after 1964, for the establishment of "trial use" alternatives to the established prayer book with the approval of the General Convention of the church.[18] Possessing authority to effect change does not equal the ability to do so effectively. How might Örsy's rules of interpretation create a matrix useful in the context of our own tradition of liturgical renewal?

Örsy emphasizes the need to consider any particular law in its broader historical and theological context. Before suggesting any liturgical change, an effective interpreter must take on the work of the historian, becoming familiar with the cultural context of the one or ones who prepared the specific text at hand, the evolution of textual meanings over time, and the dialectical context within which some texts are created. This requires the discernment of both theological foundation and core meaning. Liturgy, like law, evolves in response to historical and theological change; the ability to track the evolution of any text is essential to its interpretation. The nature of liturgical language itself can be a complicating factor in deciphering the meaning and effect of liturgical texts. It may be difficult, or impossible, to trace the development of a text because documents have been destroyed or never existed.

Liturgy is symbolic speech that protects the integrity of essential ritual elements while facilitating their expression in the context of the worshiping community. Liturgical interpretation requires discernment of the evolving mind of the worshiping Church as well as changing pastoral intentions. Interpreters of any text must guard against making the text justify a personal whim. This is particularly tempting in the creation of new liturgy, and we have many examples of liturgy that was transformed into an essentially private creation in the name of promoting some pastoral good. The same could certainly be said of canon law in the hands of drafters with a private agenda in conflict with the broader horizon of the Church. Sound interpretation, regardless of subject, requires both good rules as a guide and interpreters capable of their intelligent application—that is, not only a text to be understood, but a subject who seeks understanding.[19] Furthermore, interpretations are not infallible and eternal but evolve. This is certainly true of both law and liturgy.

One called to the vocation of interpretation benefits from a horizon that becomes increasingly broad and more expansive. As this occurs, the more the interpreter comprehends the role and context of the text at hand, the closer to the truth her or his interpretation will be. Therefore, interpretation can never be limited to any narrow field of expertise but must remain open to the richness of knowledge revealed in many disciplines. Örsy warns that "the canon lawyer who is merely a lawyer can never grasp the full meaning of ecclesiastical law."[20] Similarly, a liturgist who studies only liturgical texts can never grasp the full meaning of worship. A tolerance for ambiguity, a gift for language, faithfulness to theology and history, sensitivity to local culture and custom, and respect for legitimate diversity are the indicia of truly effective interpretation of any text; texts that bridge disciplines bring additional challenges to the task.

Örsy suggests that, because canon law is the product of our human efforts, it is imperfect; the same is true of liturgy. A reasoned process of inquiry prepares each interpreter to overcome the limitations of human language; Örsy's method provides just such a process to mediate the pastoral and theological concerns facing the Church in any context. It provides a lens through which we might view the revision of our liturgy in a new and constructive way. It is not, however, a panacea. "Legal proverbs, each containing a grain of truth but never the full truth."[21] Örsy intended his rules of interpretation as a guide, not a mandate requiring anyone's strict adherence and rigid implementation. How we might use them as tools to evaluate liturgical revision in the Episcopal Church is worthy of further inquiry.

I have intended in this essay to frame certain threshold questions, leaving the details to further and more detailed inquiry in other contexts. This is an invitation to embrace new ways of thinking and, in matters of liturgical revision, to view that enterprise not as mere rubrical "tinkering" but as a challenge to explore new horizons in the Church's life. Necessary to the entire enterprise are a commitment to preserving its theological foundation and an appreciation of the role of human reason, a concept so much a part of our Anglican integrity and self-identity.

Without doubt the Episcopal Church lives in the midst of conflicting horizons on the eve of the twenty-first century. Örsy suggests that the best solution for such a posture is to expand all conflicting horizons until the conflicts disappear in a new, broader horizon. Achieving such breadth, while preserving the integrity of the catholic faith, is the challenge we face. The answer will not be found in defining a kind of "neo-Noeticism," simply disregarding real differences in horizons in favor of an appearance of unity. Rather, we must create a milieu within which such differences may be examined critically and without acrimony in order to genuinely transcend them. Such a milieu will empower the proclamation of the gospel in a society that thinks of the Christian message as superfluous. Canon law could provide the context within which the Church, in defining its common life, enables the witness and worship of the community to be exalted, not impeded. If, as Örsy suggests, the law serves the Church's theologically defined values, then canon law and canon lawyers must embody the possibility of seeing legal norms in the broadest of contexts, discovering new answers to difficult and creative questions, helping to integrate this combination of old and new into the life of the community of all the faithful.

Today canon law in the Episcopal Church has become the almost exclusive province of civil lawyers who may have very little theological education. Curiously, many of those who advocate increased attention to canon law in the Episcopal Church omit any theological context for it. Instead, they focus principally on increasing the active participation of attorneys in parochial and diocesan legal matters, on developing means of making the canons more available, on preparing better legal commentaries on American canon law, and on establishing mechanisms for legal scholarship and study. In the process, any discussion of the theological foundation of the canon law tradition has been almost entirely obscured.

Reviving a living tradition of canon law in the Episcopal Church will require more than producing a regularly updated *White & Dykman* or founding a canon law society for Episcopalians or developing more educational opportunities to examine existing canon law (in seminaries and elsewhere). It will require us to reclaim the philosophical, theological, and historical foundations of this part of our tradition and to foster cooperation and dialogue among legal scholars, attorneys, theologians, and historians. It may require us to abandon some of our preconceived notions and to learn and borrow from other traditions. We need to abandon our comfortable prejudices, especially any fear of becoming excessively legalistic. Restoring the theological foundation in our understanding of canon law will make such legalism difficult, if not impossible, to sustain. In particular, we would do well to ask what we can learn from Roman Catholic canonists, particularly methodologically and philosophically. The Episcopal Church is heir to both Rome and Canterbury in our law and in our liturgy. Do we continue to maintain an illogical and destructive attitude to either or both which impedes the building up of our common life? If so, we need to change. We've done so very effectively in liturgical renewal; it is time to move in this direction in canon law. A living faith implies change. What might be gained by working together, learning from a common legal heritage?

Acquiring a new attitude of mind begins with new knowledge and with a willingness to adopt a new perspective. Inviting those theologically educated into dialogue with those educated in the law might bring about, to paraphrase theologian Bernard Lonergan, an enterprise that becomes "a framework for collaborative creativity."[22] It might also move us all a good deal closer to Hooker's vision of law: abiding inside the heart of God, caring for the powerless and respected by the strong, worthy of all honor, speaking with the voice of unity and concord in a disputatious world. Paul VI, in addressing the judges of the Roman rota in 1977, understood the law in terms fully consonant with Hooker's as reflecting the Church's spiritual character and informed by God's Holy Spirit.[23] Recovering such a sense of the law's vocation will enable it to become an instrument of the Church's spiritual life as well as the voice of the Church's justice. In the final analysis, this can never be intellectual enterprise alone but must be a conversion experience. It requires people of courage and perspicacity, intelligence and curiosity, creativity and humility—people whose lives have been transformed by acquiring a new attitude of mind, a *novus habitus mentis*.

Rites and Wrongs

Trite Rite: Field Notes on the Trivialization of Christian Initiation

Paul V. Marshall

MUCH OF CHRISTIAN LITURGICAL HISTORY seems to be the record of the Church's flight from the meaning of its initiatory rites. Even in our own time, when Edward Yarnold wrote of "the awe-inspiring rites of Christian initiation," he had to confess that his ancient text really said "spine-chilling rites of initiation."[1] After all, baptism in the early centuries of Christian history was a life-and-death matter—theologically, politically, and economically. It was the culmination of a process that may have cost the initiates their occupations, a process that consumed the time and energy invested in intensive catechesis and "field work" and one that perhaps saw them lose the love and respect of family and community. This was all undergone because the initiates wanted life in Christ. All of this stands in pronounced contrast to modern experience, as reported in the field notes that follow.

It is tempting to suggest that a good deal of the contemporary bumping-down of the intensity of initiatory symbolism in what remains of Christendom is related to infant baptism's status as de facto norm in all of the liturgical and many of the mainstream denominations, regardless of the positions taken in their official books. Indeed, something about the presence of infants brings out the worst, the most treacly, in many people, perhaps with good reason. Our biologically based instinct to regard recently born children as good, beautiful, innocent, and in need of our protection and nurture conflicts sharply with the idea of baptism as a necessary parting of the ways, either as a death-and-life event (Paul) or as a rebirth from one kind of life to another (John). Babies give no sign of needing that, at least not at first, and post-Enlightenment adults attribute what happens next in a child's life to nurture, almost to the exclusion of nature. A good environment, not regeneration, occupies discussions of child rearing. Thus with completely straight faces, nineteenth-century Anglicans were content to sing Clement of Alexandria's catechetical hymn "Bridle of Untamed Colts," translated as "Shepherd of Tender Youth." That point of view is alive and well.

But is infant baptism a cause of—or a victim of—the flight from spine-chilling rites where everything was at stake to happy chumming around with the shepherd of tender youth in a mutually intransitive relationship? It is probably most accurate to posit a bilateral process. Salvation without discipleship (Christendom)—the transformation of "mysteries" to be enacted into things to be received, gazed upon, or carried about (sacraments)—created a situation where costly and life-changing initiation was neither necessary nor desirable. Initiatory rites with nothing important to do (other than baptism's function as a kind of celestial fire insurance, at least in the West) became life-cycle celebrations. All this further contributed to the notion that religion was a veneer applied to the rough surfaces of a largely untransformed life.

The 1979 *Book of Common Prayer* represents an attempt to correct this situation, providing reciprocity and balance to the themes of salvation and discipleship in its initiatory rites. The Baptismal Covenant it contains is perhaps the strongest statement that the Episcopal Church has ever put forward concerning the obligations Christians take on in terms of faith and life. Just as Bishop White tolerated the language of baptismal regeneration in the liturgical text, (but himself taught quite otherwise throughout his career), there are hints that some sectors of the Church are quite uncomfortable with the serious call to a devout and holy life that the 1979 rites issue. This point is the reason for offering the "field notes" that follow.

The cases presented below are true; all come from the author's personal experience or from documents in his possession. They are reported here not because they offend the author's sensibilities (they do); they are reported because they represent the erosion of, or distraction from, the faith and experience that the several initiatory rites are meant to celebrate. It is not suggested that the persons whose actions are reported do not in any way lack faith, piety, or good intentions. However, sometimes precisely because their intentions are good, but uninformed or misinformed, they go on to create ecclesial and doctrinal anomalies, if not sacramental havoc.

The first, and most troubling, note from the field concerns a parish in a very prosperous community. The motives in this case are known with some exactness because the parish sent press releases to church periodicals. In an attempt to attract upwardly mobile young couples to their church, liturgical planners determined to allow but one child to be baptized at a service, so that each child would be, as their press release put it, "special." The eventual result of this policy was that the parish found itself having a baptism virtually every Sunday. This frequency of baptism made the planners feel a necessity to shorten the baptismal rite, and this they did—by eliminating the Baptismal Covenant, among other things.

It is no understatement to observe that in each particular this parish departed from the doctrine that the 1979 rite was expressly designed to celebrate, the confluence of death and resurrection, the beginning of new life and discipleship. Without rehashing the entire debate over "Christ and culture," it appears in this case that their first mistake foreshadows all the rest: the attempt to attract people to the Church on the culture's terms (being "special") rather than on the basis of Christ's call to "repent and believe the gospel" (Mark 1:15). As this parish explained its initiatory program, nothing about the child's life—or that of the parents and sponsors—is expected to experience significant change, except that sense of specialness (which seems rather too like the sense of being "privileged" that is so deftly lampooned in the summer camp scenes in *Addams Family Values*). The notion that baptizing children singly makes them somehow more special represents a stunning denial of what it is that happens at baptism, as a person's individuality is grafted into Christ's Body, the Church. The elimination of the Baptismal Covenant removes its uncompromising demands to fight against much of the very culture to which the parish appears to be pandering. This cheapens grace to the point where the newly baptized may be described as "special but not responsible"—privileged indeed.

This is not to deny that the Christian gospel does indeed give us an identity as children and heirs of God, does indeed thrust us in community with people who are to show Christ's love to us. Personal worth is, however, grounded in one's creation, redemption, and ongoing sanctification. Nothing can (or should try to) top that, but that is precisely what the culture of specialness constantly seeks to do.

Less harmful doctrinally, but certainly more cloying, is the somewhat more widely seen practice of the celebrant at a baptism ostentatiously cradling a newly baptized child and carrying it up and down the center aisle for oohing and aahing just before or during "Let us welcome the newly baptized" and the response that follows it. When the baby is paraded during the response, most people do not even try to join the response or pay much attention to its challenge to join in Christian discipleship. Having been present in numerous places where this practice is observed, I find several conclusions inevitable. In the same churches, the celebrant almost never walks older children or newly baptized adults through the aisle. It is not practiced for multiple baptisms. The practice is almost never visually necessary for either infants or adults. Instead, it focuses attention on how loving and caring the celebrant is, as he or she becomes the ecclesiastical version of the baby-kissing politician. Again, the rite is partially derailed by emphasizing the "specialness" of someone—in this case, the clergy. Perhaps none of this is, or is perceived to be, true. But the Peace is certainly the better time for this promenade. Then the words of welcome and invitation to share in priesthood would be undisturbed. In any event, the children would be better carried by their godparents. Also, the "Thanksgiving for the Birth or Adoption of a Child" provides an appropriate mode for acknowledging the birth of individual infants.

Clericalizing additions to initiatory rites are not restricted to the presbyterate, sad to say, although the episcopate dips its oar into the less vital waters of confirmation, reaffirmation of faith, and reception into communion. The prayer book is lucidity itself on the question of confirmation, whether we happen to agree or not.

> In the course of their Christian development, those baptized at an early age are expected, when they are ready and have been duly prepared, to make a mature public affirmation of their faith and commitment to the responsibilities of their Baptism and to receive the laying on of hands by the bishop.

> Those baptized as adults, unless baptized with laying on of hands by a bishop, are also expected to make a public affirmation of their faith and commitment to the responsibilities of their Baptism in the presence of a bishop and to receive the laying on of hands. (BCP 79, p. 412)

Those words require a mature public profession of faith made before the bishop and the laying on of the bishop's hands. Nothing could seem simpler. In the prayer book view, confirmation is not magic, nor is it by this definition unrepeatable or capable of conferring an indelible character. It is a public profession of faith by one old enough to make it knowledgeably, and it is made before the bishop as chief pastor of the diocese and representative of the universal Church, who responds with a blessing in quasi-epicletic form. Infant chrismation in Orthodoxy and childhood confirmation in Roman Catholicism are each something else intentionally. Yet more than one of our bishops chooses to deem persons who have received such rites as confirmed for Episcopalian purposes. These bishops disregard entirely the requirement for mature and public profession of faith. They also seem to understand chrism in Orthodoxy as a kind of "bishop in a bottle," whose application they apparently understand to confer not only the presence of the Spirit, whose ubiquity is a matter of dogma, but also to confer contact with the bishop, whose ubiquity is not yet an article of faith. Increasingly, bishops and diocesan committees are promulgating initiatory guidelines that treat those who have undergone educational processes and various rites called confirmation in a host of Protestant churches as having been confirmed for the purposes of this one, despite the fact that they have never confessed their faith before a bishop or received the laying on of episcopal hands. This appears to be some sort of gesture of ecumenical goodwill, but there does not seem to be much evidence of its having had any effect.

It happens that I hold no brief for confirmation. As for the compromise between the Standing Liturgical Commission and the House of Bishops represented in the 1979 book, no small number of scholars and pastors consider it absurd. However, the fact that contiguous dioceses have radically different initiatory guidelines is no great advertisement for the catholicity—or reliability—of our branch of the Church. Many bishops decry the de facto congregationalism of the Episcopal Church. Yet they do not take into account the degree to which they model parochialism by actions that imply that episcopate in Anglicanism is autocephalous, something it has never been, before or after the Reformation.

The "caring" motif detected in the lifting up, carrying about, and gazing upon children at baptism emerges again when adults are confirmed or received. Bishops have been known to bring the spouses of the newly confirmed/received up to redo a nuptial blessing *in extenso*. Or they do other kinds of household prayers with family members huddled about and leave the rest of the congregation wondering what is happening, but knowing that, whatever it is, it is special. Single and divorced members of confirmation/reception groups have been vocal about their sense of second-class citizenship, as they have no way to merit the extra episcopal attention. Another bishop announces proudly that he has "personalized" the confirmation rite and wants to "patent" his innovations involving hand-laying by sponsors along with him at confirmation. Clearly, he does not understand what his role is meant to signify (or perhaps he is unaware of a similar ritualization in the contemporary Roman rite).

The most striking example of a bishop derailing an initiatory rite in order to focus attention on himself comes from a diocesan directive requiring those confirmed or received to remain after the bishop imparts his blessing. He then removes his mitre and receives from *each* initiate a parallel hand-laying and a special blessing composed by the initiate for the occasion. Thus when a group of twenty is confirmed or received, each initiate receives one ready-made prayer book blessing. But the bishop receives twenty fresh blessings composed expressly for him, what one might call "bespoke blessings." No matter how innocent in intent, this practive suggests to a reasonable onlooker that the bishop suffers from an insatiable ego or else from a catastrophic need for blessing that the assembly is there to serve, at the cost of its common prayer.

As a group, these initiatory problems represent capitulation to a culture of specialness. They speak a theology in which a caring attitude has displaced personal responsibility as the chief virtue and principal homiletical theme.

Liturgical revisers must ask themselves, have the rites themselves no power to make their point in such a way as to preclude such anomalies? Is there a liturgical solution to the problem here? The answer to both questions, empirically, is no. The only hope would be for clergy, aspiring clergy, and other planners of liturgy to encounter the rites celebrated with integrity and in their fullness. We have no continuing education requirement in the clerical vocation in the Episcopal Church (as there is in the Presbyterian, for example). So we cannot insure that clergy even understand the rites that have appeared since they took canonical examinations. Additionally, there is manifest foolishness in suggesting the adoption of rubrics indicating what cannot be done. Such a move would invite the passive-aggressive invention of even odder mutations.

It is axiomatic that institutions tend to take on the characteristics of their leaders. The problems I have recounted in the celebration of the primary initiation, baptism, and the secondary rite, confirmation, may evade solution until we attend to the problems in a tertiary initiatory rite: ordination. We are not accustomed to speaking of ordination or religious profession as initiation, and there are sound reasons for keeping them in a different category. However, from an anthropological standpoint, they have a high initiatory quotient, and in that sense they are discussed here.

People sometimes fault ordinations for having more elaborate ceremony than baptisms. It is tempting to agree with such a position. True enough, baptism is the primary sacrament. And certainly, ordinations occasionally get out of hand. However, a similar leveling anticlericalism frequently distorts an entirely appropriate interest in empowering lay ministry. The disagreement over baptism vs. ordination would not arise, however, if both baptism and ordination were observed as celebrations of the Church and the Spirit, a leveling up for once.

There is no reason why parochial or regional quarterly celebrations of baptism (and confirmation/reception/reaffirmation) should not be enormously rich affairs. There is equally little reason why quarterly ordinations should not be enormously rich affairs as well. The trick in either case is to keep the focus on the Church as it grows in baptism and as it recognizes the perpetuation of its leadership in matters of Word and Sacrament in ordination. A shift in spirituality would occur if people were usually baptized in groups and if candidates were ordained in cathedral or regional liturgies. This would go a long way toward replacing unproductive notions of "specialness" with a fruitful apprehension of the corporate nature of the Church.

I have spent the better part of two decades in the training of ordinands. I have found that the people who believe they may be called to ordained ministry are shaped in a certain way by our preordination procedures. They become passive-aggressive wrecks with weak egos, persons in need of constant reassurance of their worth. The number of screening committees intoxicated with the feeling of power is truly shocking. I routinely advise students how to answer the clichéd question "What could you do as an ordained person that you can't do as a lay person?" I tell them to count to ten before answering and to pray for strength not to make remarks about the inanity and near-heresy of such a question. Certainly we are to prefer those few who want to *do* the work of a bishop, priest, or deacon to those many obsessed with the desire to *be* or to *be chosen* for those offices. Nonetheless, the question implies that ordination is about getting to do certain things, getting power for oneself. But, in fact, preparation for holy orders is largely about offering to place oneself under orders, submitting to a discipline and to an accountability from which lay people are entirely free in Anglicanism. Missing this key theological point so early in the preordination process may push an ordinand toward a career that emphasizes self rather than ministry in and for the Church. The preordination process continues in an adversarial role in so many dioceses. All too often, this makes the successful (or merely persistent) candidates consider ordination rather than ministry as the pot of gold at the end of the seminary rainbow. The large percentage of students who become fixated on what they routinely call "my priesthood" is at once both appalling and understandable. That ordination should become one more occasion for self-expression is not hard to understand, given the nature of the process leading up to it. A Roman Catholic friend, used to seeing deacons and priests ordained only in groups at a cathedral liturgy, observed some years ago the ordination of a mutual friend. He remarked that ordinations to the priesthood in the Episcopal Church resemble coronations.

Ordinations should be celebrations of the entire Church. By and large, we are better at this when making ordinations to the episcopate and the diaconate. Those to the presbyterate all too often are worthy of my friend's complaints. To escape coronation syndrome and to re-establish the experience of the presbyterate as an ecclesial and collegial office, bishops must modify the excesses they permit candidates to perpetrate at ordinations. Furthermore, if we are to re-emphasize the primary collegiality of a bishop—that maintained with the presbyters of the diocese more than with the other members of an episcopal caste or club—then we must plan and enact all of the ordination rites so that they appear to be and are experienced as acts of and for the whole Church.

Lest a reader believe that the apparently hungry egos of clergy are not a liturgical problem, consider two final field notes. One concerns a priest; another concerns a bishop. At a recent "Celebration of a New Ministry," the newly instituted priest decreed that, in each of the churches in the yoked arrangement for which she was assuming responsibility, the altar was to be adorned with a teddy bear, whenever she was presiding at the liturgy. This would be the symbol of her ministry, which especially related to children. Note that the teddy bear was to appear only when she was present. The liturgy in these churches was not primarily understood as that of the Church; it was that of the priest, marked by this peculiar piece of *fermentum*.

It should be noted that the rite for the institution of new ministries invites abuse, an invitation that is seldom left unaccepted. The presence of the bishop, the presentation, the use of the litany for ordinations, and above all, the presentation of symbols of office—all these work together to produce an experience that can become half ordination and half coronation. The fact that the new minister often comes into the church in alb only and is vested with stole and chasuble during the induction certainly gives the impression that what is being celebrated is ordination. The rubric permitting the presentation of other symbols besides books, keys, oil, and so forth offers an often irresistible temptation to be cute. That the porrection of instruments properly belongs to ordination in the first place, seems to matter little. This portion of the institution service has seen in the past few months the giving of everything from clown noses (mimicking a recent episcopal consecration) to fishing tackle. Again, a rite is derailed in dioceses where institutions compete to see which will outdo the others in this form of creativity, and the emphasis of the service shifts accordingly.

As to the other example, a bishop has written to his priests that he is "reviving" what he believes to be an ancient oriental analog to the stole, as a vestment for bishops only. (Actually, it has never gone out of use in the Eastern churches.) He argues that therefore each order of ministry would have its "own" stole—once again, something special. In the West, the basic form of deacon's, priest's, and bishop's stole is the same—the difference is the number of shoulders it drapes. The bishop's need to differentiate himself from his presbyters ignores the evolution of the stole worn on both shoulders in the West: the common vestment of the college that is the bishop and the presbyters. On this matter the testimony of the ancient West is quite clear. Beyond that, the Eastern garment requires the rest of the eastern vestments to make symbolic— and sartorial—sense.

In each of these cases, we see the need of an individual to stand out in the Church—not by faithfulness, pious example, or loving service but by an external mark of "special" identity.

I have argued elsewhere that the *lex orandi–lex credendi* relationship, as Anglicans usually portray it, requires careful re-examination. However, we need a disciplined effort to celebrate initiatory rites at the three levels observed here—in a way that emphasizes their ecclesial, christological, and communal nature. We must also recast the language of the ordination rites. Together these efforts can go a long way toward moving our ecclesial experience from a culture of self-obsession to the far more significant counterculture of shared discipleship.

Baptism: Rite of Inclusion or Exclusion?

Linda Moeller

LITURGICAL REVISION THAT CLAIMS to be anything beyond cosmetic change must begin by asking the hard questions. The questions then have to be addressed in the light of Scripture, tradition, and reason. One such question is presently being asked by some parishes scattered throughout the Church. They are asking about the relationship of two Sacraments, baptism and eucharist, and about all that is implied by their relationship. By opening the eucharistic table to the unbaptized, these parishes are asking how the Episcopal Church understands baptism and eucharist. Instead of a gateway to new life, these churches see baptism as a barrier to inclusivity; a barrier they intend to remove by opening the table to all who would approach.

"First join the club, then join us at the table. Celebrate now, sign up later."[1] In two simple sentences the *New York Times* has expressed the range of opinion on the ecclesiology, sacramental theology, and liturgical practice involved in this discussion. The article goes on to state that some parishes believe that, by removing any restrictions on who may receive the Body and Blood at the table, they are returning to the roots of and being more faithful to the intention of the primitive Church. Currently, at least one church has been designed, built, and its worship structured to embody the "table-to-font" as opposed to the "font-to-table" side of the discussion. While presently a minority, such parishes agree with the sacramental theology expressed by the new building: that there is something in the Church's exclusive policies concerning baptism/eucharist that creates a real impediment to faith and ministry.

The two Sacraments in question are essential to the self-identification of the Episcopal Church as Reformed and catholic. The relationship between baptism and eucharist is at the core of how Episcopalians understand themselves to stand in the catholic tradition while exhibiting the finest theological and liturgical foundations laid by the Reformers.

The foundation of that Reformed church is a catholic church in possession of a historical and continuous tradition of faith and practice that is
orthodox as distinct from either schismatic or heretical.[2] Does the tradition as revealed by texts support changing our practice of baptism before
eucharist in order to be less exclusive? Would the title of Reformed and
catholic still be a valid description should a change be made in
baptismal/eucharistic practice?

We must examine Scripture, the tradition as recorded in the documents, and the theology that is lived out in the liturgy. Based on that
examination, we must decide if an individual should come to the Lord's
Table through the waters of baptism or whether the eucharistic table
fellowship should be the motivation that moves one to the font. And if
the change should be deemed necessary, would it solve the problem of
exclusivism or simply hide the pain, masking the real problem?

The scope of this essay will not permit a full exploration of all the
supporting arguments for both sides of this debate. But one issue must
be named and dealt with before we enter the discussion. In the
Constitution and Canons of the Episcopal Church, Title I Canon 17 section
7 states that "[N]o unbaptized person shall be eligible to receive Holy
Communion in this Church." The canons, while voted on and encoded
by human beings, are the rules we have agreed will govern our common
life. Certainly not unchangeable, they are, however, not easily changed. If
change is a possibility, much work must be done. The Church must
examine all the resources, paying close attention to the working of the
Holy Spirit in the Church and seeking understanding. At the same time
the Church must carefully avoid the seduction of relevancy as an accommodation to the present time. The pursuit of relevancy at the expense of
the integrity of worship may make our liturgy become merely a means to
an end rather than an opportunity to encounter God.

TABLE-TO-FONT

THE TABLE-TO-FONT APPROACH to the Sacraments would make welcome
all who desire to participate in the eucharist, regardless of their
baptismal state. Although this issue has not appeared on the agendas of
many of the Church's liturgical commissions, this is precisely the time to
discuss it. Now is the time to sort out theology from emotion, thought-
out responses from instinctual, time-conditioned reactions. The decision

should be made in a climate of pastoral, theological, and academic reason that will allow the voice of God to be heard.

The advocates of the table-to-font approach claim that they are more closely approximating the action and intent of the Church in its earliest form. They believe that they have journeyed back to the earliest days of the Church and have faithfully translated that ritual life. The first question we must ask ourselves is this: How did the earliest Christians understand what they were doing when they shared in the breaking of the Bread?

Paul's admonitions to the Corinthians inform us that the earliest Christian eucharist was a complete meal. This meal was closely associated with the first Christian's experience of Jesus' own ministry—a ministry often expressed in an environment of table-fellowship. The *meal* provided Christians with the connecting link between their own experience of Easter faith and of the ministry of Jesus.

The Easter faith of the disciples grew from their perception of Jesus' message, a message of forgiveness of sins and a new covenant with God. "This was symbolized by a table-fellowship... of such joy and gladness that it survived the crucifixion and provided the focal point for the community life of the earliest Christians."[3]

For the early disciples, the meal that would become the eucharist carried at least two meanings. One meaning was eschatological: The meal signaled the presence of the kingdom Jesus had proclaimed even before it has fully arrived. The other meaning was reconciliatory: The meal signaled the forgiveness of sins and the possibility of that new relationship with God and others that was central to Jesus' own preaching. The meal was a direct link with the earthly ministry of Jesus that the disciples had personally experienced, as well as the bond of the community that had been shaped around the person of Jesus. For this reason meals play a central role in the Easter stories. When he walked with humanity, "Jesus used the ministry of the table as a central feature in his proclamation of God's forgiveness."[4]

The community's meal, their eucharist, quickly became an extension of Jesus' ministry and message, especially to those who were marginalized by the society. The common experiences of conversion and forgiveness offered by Jesus would have made it unimportant for the earliest believers to distinguish rigorously between a eucharistic meal and an ordinary community meal. Whenever the community of believers assembled to break bread, it experienced the presence of the Risen One who offers "forgiveness of sins" (Acts 10:34-43).

There can be little doubt that conversion, forgiveness, and table-fellowship were inextricably linked together for the early Church. Another aspect of the table-fellowship, frequently overlooked today but ingrained in the very being of first-century people, was hospitality. Ideas about hospitality would later contribute to the eucharistic tradition of the Church. Table-fellowship and hospitality were both essential to the culture and society in which Jesus lived and moved. His was a world in which hospitality and the sacred bond between guest and host were seen as the moral foundations upon which the universe stood.[5] Hospitality to the stranger was central to first-century life.

The impressions we get from Scripture tend to leave us thinking that *meal* and *gospel* are inseparable. Meals were times of hospitality set apart from the activities and possible hostilities of everyday life. They were sacred times when individuals would recognize their common bond as children of the Creator. Nowhere do any of the stories in the Scripture mention participation in the meal being restricted to the baptized.

It is in the incredibly strong link between table-fellowship, hospitality, Jesus' ministry, conversion, and forgiveness that the proponents of an "open" eucharist base their claims. For are we not all ultimately dependent on the grace of God, that undeserved free gift? In the stories we have of Jesus' ministry, Jesus didn't wait for the people to repent of misdeeds before he offered them acceptance and forgiveness. Instead, Jesus made the first approach, taking the initiative, offering friendship. Eucharist, "thanksgiving," is the only appropriate response to that grace.

FONT-TO-TABLE

CHRISTIAN BAPTISM AS AN INITIATORY RITE made its appearance simultaneously with the Christian community's birth. Luke's account of the Day of Pentecost tells us of the normative sequence: "So those who received his word were baptized, and there were added that day about three thousand souls. And they devoted themselves to the apostles' teaching and fellowship, to the breaking of bread and the prayers" (Acts 2:41-42). New Testament scholars may disagree on what words may actually be attributed to Jesus. But we do know that the authors of both Mark and Matthew understood baptism to be so important as to include this in the closing lines: "Go therefore and make disciples of all nations, baptizing them in the name of the Father and of the Son and of the Holy Spirit" (Matt. 28:19) and "Go into all the world and proclaim the good news to the whole creation. The one who believes and is baptized will be saved" (Mark 16:15b-16a). The text leaves no doubt about the significance that the first Christians attributed to this rite of initiation. Converts were first given new life in baptism, and then that new life was nourished at the table. The first Christians valued the table ministry of Jesus but did not confuse that ministry with the eucharistic meal of the Church.

Paul would probably have said that for redeemed children of God, nothing is forbidden but not everything is helpful. "Love, to Paul, [was] constant concern for the church, for one's brothers and sisters, for one's fellow Christians,"[6] and further, "love allows for not insisting on one's integrity at the expense of the unity of the community."[7]

The first Christians understood that participation in the sacramental ritual of baptism was the way an individual became a Christian. "All who were not already laity by baptism... even those who were already convinced of the truth of the gospel but had not yet received [the] sacrament—were invariably turned out before prayer of any kind was offered, let alone the eucharist."[8] The early Church functioned under the premise that "the world had a right to hear the gospel; but those who [had] not yet 'put on Christ' by baptism (Gal 3:27)... [could] not join in offering that prevailing prayer. All who had not entered the order of the laity were therefore without exception turned out of the assembly after the sermon...[9] [I]t was only to those who received baptism that the church offered either remission of sins or eternal salvation."[10]

In the earliest Christian documents and in the later documents that Anglicans claim to be descriptive of Anglicanism, it is clear that "throughout history, the church has insisted that the Eucharist is for the baptized." The intention is not to discriminate against or embarrass individuals who may be sincere but unbaptized; the purpose of the restriction is to indicate that the Lord's Supper is distinctive, set apart from other forms of eating and drinking. The ecclesiology inherent in the insistence on membership before eucharist is one of a community that finds itself in the world but set apart from it: a holy community. In that community the Lord's Supper, by being reserved to members of the Body of Christ (i.e. the Church) becomes a "holy" communion.

The Supper is to be seen as more than a social gathering; those who come to the Lord's Table should recognize him in the breaking of bread, find in him the source of life, and be joined in unity with him and one another. Baptism signifies precisely the enlightenment, the gift of divine life, and the incorporation into the community of faith that makes true eucharistic joy possible.[11]

Both the *Didache* and the *Apostolic Tradition* are quite clear in their understanding of the relationship between baptism and eucharist. The *Didache* simply states, "And let none eat or drink of your eucharist, but they that are baptized into the name of the Lord."[12]

The *Apostolic Tradition* is no less clear: "catechumens ought not to sit at table with the faithful A catechumen shall not sit at table at the Lord's Supper."[13] "And let all take care that no unbaptized person taste of the eucharist."[14]

Whenever a rule is written forbidding an activity, we may surmise that the activity was taking place somewhere. Nevertheless, it is quite clear from the *Apostolic Tradition* that the early Church had a definite sense of how the two Sacraments should relate to each other. From their admission to the catechumenate, individuals would attend the mass of the catechumens "but were not allowed to associate themselves with the prayers of the faithful or the kiss of peace, still less the eucharist itself."[15]

There is no dearth of patristic evidence to support, not only the practice of baptism before eucharist, but also the theology that was the foundation of that pattern.

In his *First Apology*, Justin wrote:

and this food is called eucharist by us, of which no one else is allowed to partake than those who believe the things taught by us to be true, and who are washed with the washing for the forgiveness of sins and for rebirth.... For we do not receive these things as common food and common drink.[16]

Justin's writing explained that it was teaching and the waters of baptism that together yielded a community that gathered for the uncommon meal and that it was baptism that always led to the shared meal.

The voices that echo from the apostolic and patristic eras of the Christian Church are important to modern Episcopalians. In the authority attested to by the choir of their combined voices, we find the evidence of the Spirit working in the Church. There is not a single powerful voice but a community that speaks in authority.

The Anglican divine Richard Hooker (1554-1600) left no room to debate his understanding of either the Sacraments or just how one became a member of the Body of Christ. When reading *On the Laws of Ecclesiastical Polity* (1594-97), one cannot ignore Hooker's frequent references to the community that is a unified Body, the Church. Mr. Hooker wrote:

> The unity of which visible body and Church of Christ consisteth in that uniformity which all several persons thereunto belonging have, by reason of that one Lord whose servants they all profess themselves, that one Faith which they all acknowledge, that one Baptism wherewith they are all initiated. (Book III, Chap. I.3)

> [Entered we are not into the visible Church before our admittance by the door of Baptism. (Book III Ch. I.6)

In Book V, Chapter 67, there is no mistaking Hooker's intent regarding the Sacraments of baptism and eucharist. His very simple statement is, "No man therefore receiveth this sacrament [Sacrament of the Body and Blood of Christ] before Baptism, because no dead thing is capable of nourishment."

The question of font first or table first finds its origins, not in our theology, ecclesiology, or liturgical practice, but in the end products of the Enlightenment and the pop psychology of the twentieth century. We are much more comfortable with columns that add up, experiments that can be reproduced, or recommendations for esteem-enhancing behavior. We are much happier if we can explain in a legalistic manner the exact moment of salvation, who is saved, and when it happened.

The rugged individualism that is so prominent in the American understanding of self has also taken its toll on the way we live out our faith. The importance, indeed centrality, of community for Christians has been hidden by an egocentric outlook on life. As a result of the changing societal dynamics that have been carried into the Church from the world, we have lost our sense of the mystery of salvation, real presence, Sacrament, and Church. "Thus, baptism is seen, not as a dynamic activity of Christ through which the gospel comes to us, but as a mechanical action of the church."[17]

Baptism is often looked upon as a social superstition, something that has to be done to keep the grandparents happy, or as a procedure that will impart a legal status with God. In an effort to realize relevance, we have sacrificed the understanding of baptism as the beginning of a covenental relationship between the newly baptized and God — baptism as a rite that has to do with the Church catholic. We no longer emphasize baptism as

> [t]he rite of initiation that brings us into covenant with God and into the community of the covenant where the promises and claims of God are set before us continually. We seem to have forgotten [that] baptism sets into motion a dynamic of life that defies legal precision or even clear definition... [and that] it is an act principally for the Church. The whole Church in faith and spirit enters the cleansing stream.[18]

Clearly, a direct relationship exists between the Sacraments of baptism and eucharist. The first eucharistic meal shared with the community was, historically and theologically, the climax and completion of the Easter baptisms. Our present *Book of Common Prayer* assumes that the eucharist will be the concluding ritual action of the baptismal liturgy.

> The eucharist is, in one sense, the final repeatable act of the sacrament of Christian initiation. The bond established between the Christian and the dying and rising Christ in baptism is renewed week after week by Christians' common participation in the eucharist and communion with one another in the Body of Christ. Conversely, the interrelation of

baptism and eucharist and their coinherence in the Paschal
Mystery are obscured unless those who are baptized participate
in the eucharist and receive communion.[19]

The Church of the twentieth century finds itself facing incredible opportunity to spread the gospel to a post-Christian world that desperately
needs to hear the Good News. It is a time to explore new ways to share
the gospel with those who have not heard it, to live out the welcome of
Christ. When we hear of a church that has flung wide its door, its arms,
and its eucharistic table to all who would come, our first reaction might
be one of assent. Immediate pictures come to mind of Jesus as he sat at
table with his friends, of the thousands who listened to the Sermon on
the Mount and later ate fish and bread, of the intimate atmosphere in the
home of Martha and Mary. On further consideration, however, we must
not forget the reality of a Church that is called to be the Body of Christ in
this world, recognizing the responsibility and stewardship that are ours.
    It is surely possible for an individual to come to a mature and abid-
ing faith in God and in God's Son, Jesus Christ, by first approaching the
table upon which the meal celebrates our salvation. In fact, it is contrary
to Christian theology to limit the working of the Holy Spirit to the
confines of a specific Sacrament. The risk, however, lies in the alternative
possibility: that many more would develop an intensely private, personal
Christianity to the exclusion of the community that is the Church and
the heavily communal aspect of the eucharistic meal? Would they ever
experience the bond of Christian unity, no matter how flawed that unity
might be?
    Faith implies community. For "although its subject is always the
person, faith is never individualistic, for it is directed to that which is
revealed to it as absolute truth, which by its very nature is incapable of
being individual."[20] An open eucharistic table encourages "religious feeling" over faith, and religious feeling is the antithesis of faith. Religious
feeling is "utterly individualistic, feels itself to be inexpressible and shies
away from expression and comprehension ... and easily accepts a rupture
between religion and life."[21] A Church that would recognize eucharist as
an incorporating Sacrament over and against baptism has lost sight of
one of the primary characteristics of the early Church and the first
Christians: community. The primitive Church was before all else the

Body of Christ made up of its various members.

In an effort to be welcoming and unifying by placing no restrictions on the reception of the eucharist, we would replace the Church as a source and gift of unity from above with the Church as the expression of a earthly, natural unity from below.[22] Isolating the eucharist into a self-sufficient activity reveals a eucharistic theology that attempts to translate the language of theology into the language of today. It is a theology that is "unaware of the eucharist as above all a sacrament of the Church, as the gift and fulfillment of that unity of faith and love, communion of the one Spirit in which the essence of the Church is revealed."[23] In the "new" language of eucharistic theology, the eucharist is no longer the Sacrament *par excellence* of *corpus Christi*, the unique sharing of community members and their communion with God. In it, instead, communion and union with each other have become a "particular, individual means of personal sanctification to which each resorts or from which each abstains according to the measure of his [sic] personal and self-understood 'spiritual needs,' frame of mind, preparation or unpreparation."[24]

In our very human efforts to create unity, we have redefined the source of that unity, wresting it from God and ensconcing it in humans. We have erected an idol to unity and made it the end that justifies the means. No longer is God "its source, content and goal... Unity, which is *from* God, has ceased to be unity with God and in God, who alone fulfills it as genuine unity and genuine life. Unity becomes its own content, its own 'God.'"[25]

CONCLUSION

THOSE WHO WOULD INVITE THE UNBAPTIZED to the table have identified valid concerns about the Episcopal Church and its liturgy. Has it become an exclusive, inhospitable institution that places more value on the letter of the law than the spirit of the law? Has our liturgy contributed to the confusion rather than shedding light in a troubled time? The key is a twofold approach to the way we, as a Church, live out our faith: (1) restoration and strengthening of ministries already in place, rather than transposition of the dominical Sacraments; and (2) revaluing a ministry of welcome, hospitality, and evangelism and restoring baptismal formation and discipline. In addition to the individual healing and growth that would result from such a program, Christians could hope to gain a Church composed of disciples rather than customers, because its members have undergone a process of re-socialization, and a Church which is less an accepted social institution in a service-oriented economy than a quasi-society in its own right, the breeder of a genuine subculture that is capable of questioning the values and assumptions of the world around it.[26]

Perhaps the greatest contribution made by recent liturgical revision, as embodied in the 1979 *Book of Common Prayer,* is the progress toward the restoration of, not only the rite, but the understanding of baptism. Our present prayer book and its rite for Holy Baptism contains all the necessary tools needed to complete the journey. We still have much to do, however, if we are to triumph over the many false starts.

Over the years baptism was replaced by ordination as the Sacrament that made "real" Christians. The 1979 prayer book rite for baptism begins with an Opening Acclamation and the baptismal acclamation in a versicle and response form. It then proceeds with the Ministry of the Word in a manner identical to the familiar Sunday eucharistic service. An ordination, on the other hand, has the Presentation and Litany before the start of the Ministry of the Word. The Lessons for an ordination are specially selected, though they may be the Lessons of the day. The Lessons for a baptism could also be chosen with special attention to baptismal imagery, perhaps taken from the Lessons used during the Easter Vigil. The postcommunion prayer at an ordination carries on with the special tone of the rite, but the postcommunion prayer at a baptism returns to the "standard" eucharistic postcommunion prayer. From the very beginning, an ordination is, without a doubt, a special event. There is much more room for speculation at the beginning of and during a baptism. As the service is presently laid out, the actual baptism is easily seen as something "stuck into" the center of a eucharistic service, instead of the eucharist being a culmination of the baptismal event. Until we are willing to accord special attention to the rite of initiation, recognizing the import of the life change that accompanies the new birth in baptism, can we truly be surprised that it is undervalued by those new to the tradition? We attempt to make the liturgy easy for participants not accustomed to a primary liturgical role. But in doing so we have simplified what should be highlighted and combined elements (i.e., presentation and examination) that should stand on their own.

We have also managed to divorce the sense of congregants' recommitment to their own baptismal vows from the welcoming of the newest member(s) of the community. The ritual pattern now used interrupts the congregants' affirmation of their own baptisms with the baptism about to take place. Separating the Baptismal Covenant from the water bath by the Prayers for the Candidates and the Thanksgiving over the Water breaks the momentum that impels us to rush forward to the water bath, whether for the first time or in remembrance of a previous bath. Once again, this implies a separation of the baptismal event from the communal life of the congregation, and it underscores an interpretation of baptism as secondary to the primary service of eucharist.

In the pluralistic age of the twentieth century, the Episcopal Church has to address its reputation, deserved or not, for exclusivism and elitism. The abrogation of traditional sacramental theology and ecclesiology is not the answer. It simply changes the focus of that exclusivism from the eucharistic table to the baptismal font. Opening the table to all, in fact, creates a new elite, nuanced by gnosticism, of those who move beyond the table to become baptized members of the Body of Christ.

Over the centuries, the road that leads us to the eucharistic table through the waters of the font may have become overgrown. It may, indeed, seem impassable at times. What is required, however, is not a new road but the clearing of the existing path. The Church already owns the tools—perhaps a bit rusty from neglect. But these tools can accomplish its purposes: the ministry of hospitality and the catechumenate. It is with its own tools that the Church can repair the breach caused by exclusivism and elitism.

The Already But Not Yet: Musings on the Future Revision of the Ordination Rite for Bishops

Richard G. Leggett

AS A SEMINARIAN IN THE LATE SEVENTIES and early eighties I was introduced by William Petersen, then professor of church history at Nashotah House, to the case study approach to the Church in history. By focusing on specific cases rather than on a global survey, students explored the issues and personalities that had shaped the Church's life over the centuries. In the spirit of a case study, I offer some reflections on the future revision of the rite for the ordination of a bishop, rather than making a more extensive critique of the entire ordinal. Many of my comments apply equally well to the rites for the ordination of presbyters and deacons, but it seems good to me at this time to focus solely on the ordination rite of a bishop.

Let me set the context first. The postwar years have been a period of great change in the character of the Anglican communion. Events have shaped our liturgical life in ways that were unimaginable fifty years ago. In 1947 the Church of South India came into being, bringing a new liturgical tradition, consciously ecumenical, consciously the child of the liturgical movement of the early twentieth century, and consciously Indian in ethos. Its liturgical rites influenced liturgical revision throughout the English-speaking world and eventually provided the basic shape of the present ordinal.[1]

The second momentous occasion to influence liturgical revision among Anglicans was the Second Vatican Council, with its appropriation of many of the principles of the liturgical movement in the Constitution on the Sacred Liturgy. In 1968 the new Roman rite for the ordination of bishops, presbyters, and deacons appeared. This liturgical text has affinities to certain aspects of the South Indian ordinal, especially in the threefold shape of the ordination prayers. The Roman rites as well as others loom in the background of the 1970 trial use ordinal of the Episcopal Church.[2]

The 1970 ordinal (influenced by the Church of South India) the Anglican-Methodist unity proposals in Great Britain, and the Roman rites of 1968 marked a major step forward in the celebration of ordination.[3] All three rites follow a parallel structure and terminology for the key elements. New and more conspicuous roles appear for the laity. The ordination prayers are full of powerful imagery, and the laying on of hands with its accompanying petition for the gift of the Holy Spirit takes place within the context of these prayers.

We now face, however, the possibility of further liturgical revision, and well we should. In the quarter of a century since the trial use ordinal appeared, American Anglicanism has undergone significant change. Our renewed emphasis on Christian initiation has succeeded in raising up a generation or more of the faithful who believe that one is *baptized* into ministry and ordained into order. The ordained ministry, in all three orders, has opened to women. This has put new stress on our liturgical language and brought many of us to a new awareness of the power of language to wound as well as heal. In this context, further liturgical revision seems not only desirable but necessary.

Among the rites in need of further revision is the rite for the ordination of a bishop. We stand in the light of the ordination of women to the episcopate and at the threshold of full communion with the Evangelical Lutheran Church in America. Now we must ask, "Does the present rite for the ordination of a bishop express our theology of the episcopate?" An honest answer is, "Not yet."

THE PRESENTATION OF THE BISHOP-ELECT

SURPRISINGLY, THE RITE MAKES NO EXPLICIT PROVISION for deacons to be among the presenters of the bishop-elect.[4] In contrast, the 1985 Canadian ordinal specifies that the presenters of the bishop-elect are to be "representatives of the diocese and province (priests, deacons, and lay persons)."[5] Given our renewed sense of the relationship between the bishop and the deacons of a diocese, the inclusion of deacons among the presenters of the bishop-elect would be a visible sign of "the special ministry of servanthood" they exercise under the bishop's authority.[6]

Although the litany has been a consistent feature of Anglican ordination rites since the first ordinal in 1550, its continued presence is not unquestionable. Paul Bradshaw has argued that the litany was understood by the Reformers as the requisite public prayer.[7] Its petition for the grace of the Holy Spirit for the exercise of the office was the essential public prayer in the first and subsequent ordinals. If so, then we must ask what role the litany now plays in a rite that has an ordination prayer with a specific petition for the gift of the Holy Spirit.

One may be tempted to argue that the litany is the prayer of the faithful. But this argument runs aground on the period of silence preceding the ordination prayer itself. This is clearly the intent of the South Indian ordinal: "The Moderator calls the people to silent prayer."[8] In a similar vein, the New Zealand rite of 1989 calls for the presiding bishop to bid the people as follows: "Like the first disciples waiting for your coming, empowering Spirit, we watch and pray. *The congregation prays in silence for the bishop-elect.*"[9]

Another tack is to consider the litany analogous to the prayers for the candidates in baptism. In this case, then, the present litany may be too lengthy for use. In the 1970 trial use rite, "A Litany for the Ministry of the Church" was proposed.[10] Rather than replicating the prayers of the faithful at the eucharist, this litany was shorter and more focused on the ministry of the Church. It might provide a model for future revision. As mentioned above, however, several recent revisions of the ordinal have emphasized the period of silent prayer before the ordination prayer and either omitted the litany or made the recitation of a litany optional.[11]

THE READINGS

SCRIPTURE CAN BE USED IN VARIOUS WAYS in liturgical rites. Among these purposes, at least four can be discerned: (1) didactic, (2) anamnetic, (3) paracletic, and (4) doxological.[12] The didactic purpose is characterized by lectio continua and the exposition of the readings in the liturgical assembly. The second, anamnetic, is closely related to the first but sees the readings as "celebrating, interpreting and stimulating the liturgical action itself."[13]

The paracletic use of the Scriptures flows from the first two. In this approach the readings are chosen primarily for pastoral rather than educational or liturgical reasons, meeting the needs of the particular community gathered for the liturgical action.[14] In the final approach, doxological, the primary purpose of reading the Scriptures is to offer glory to God rather than to benefit the listeners perse.[15] When the readings are read in a language not known to the congregation or without attention being paid to whether the people can hear, understand, or use what is being read, then the purpose of the readings is doxological.[16]

In the Anglican tradition, the readings for the ordination of a bishop have tended to be anamnetic in purpose. That is, the readings illuminate the purpose of the occasion and, in some cases, connect the order being conferred with certain key events in the community's past. When we consider the rubric in the present ordinal, this is clearly the intent of the compilers.

> The Readings are ordinarily selected from the following list and may be lengthened if desired. On a Major Feast or on a Sunday, the Presiding Bishop may select Readings from the Proper of the Day.[17]

I suggest that this rubric is problematic in at least two ways.

First, both of the texts from Isaiah appointed for the ordination of a bishop have messianic associations and are not necessarily descriptive of the Church's expectations of its bishops.[18] Psalm 99, a kingship psalm appointed for the ordination of a bishop, raises various specters, including the appropriateness of associating the ministry of bishops with monarchy.[19] Psalm 40:1-14, also appointed for the ordination of bishops, is a plea for vindication by one who has experienced persecution and rejection at the hands of those among whom the psalmist has ministered.[20]

When we look at the Epistles, we note that in Heb. 5:1-10 the author compares and contrasts the Aaronic high priest with Christ the High Priest. Do we wish to associate the ministry of a bishop with that of a high priest? Despite the antiquity of the image in historic liturgical texts, we need to question seriously whether this image adequately reflects our experience of the bishop as one who is called "to be in all things a faithful pastor and wholesome example for the entire flock of Christ."[21]

In short, the present list of appointed readings for the ordination of a bishop contains those that propose a scriptural typology for the ministry of a bishop that does not conform to the image of episcopal ministry laid out elsewhere in the rite. Incorporation into the high priestly ministry of Jesus Christ is accomplished by baptism, not by ordination.[22] The whole People of God, not only the ordained, are charged with being witnesses and signs to the messianic reign of Jesus Christ. When we choose readings for the ordination of a bishop, we must carefully avoid asking more of the bishop-elect than God asks.

Second, the present selection of readings does not include texts that associate women with the earliest apostolic ministry. True, when the ordinal first appeared, the ordination of women to the episcopate was remote in the minds of many. But it is our present reality. This is not a case of special pleading for one group among many; it is a call for us to insure that the whole story of the early apostolic ministry is told and that the role of women in the spread of the gospel is remembered. If the bishop is "to be one with the apostles in proclaiming Christ's resurrection," then why do we not have the story of Mary Magdalene, the first witness to the Resurrection?[23] If the bishop is "to testify to Christ's sovereignty as Lord of lords and King of kings," then why do we not have the story of Martha of Bethany, who confessed Christ as "the Messiah, the Son of God, the one coming into the world"?[24] The list could go on: Lydia, in whose home the church at Philippi began,[25] Damaris in Athens and Priscilla in Corinth,[26] and all those mentioned by Paul at the conclusion of Romans as his colleagues in the apostolic work.[27]

It is difficult to produce a list that will satisfy all or do justice to all the dimensions of episcopal ministry. This difficulty leads me to suggest that the way forward in future revision is to set aside our preference for a list of appointed readings and, as we do for baptism, to appoint the readings of the day as those for the ordination. This possibility is given as an option in the present rubric. It would be a step forward if the next ordinal adopted the Canadian rubric: "The prayers, readings, and preface are normally those of the day."[28]

THE EXAMINATION OF THE BISHOP-ELECT

IN TRUTH, THE EXAMINATION IS NOT a test that the bishop-elect can pass or fail. It is a statement of the Church's expectations of the bishop-elect in the conduct of her or his ministry. To this the bishop-elect is asked to consent. In this regard it has more in common with the Baptismal Covenant and perhaps, in future revisions, should be entitled "The Covenant of Ministry" or, as it is in the New Zealand revision, "The

Commitment."[29]

One of the strengths of the New Zealand text is its inclusion of a promise made by the bishop-elect to exercise her or his authority collegially.

Presiding Bishop Will you uphold the authority of the General Synod and the Constitution of the Church of this Province?

Bishop-elect Yes, I will. I am under that authority, and will exercise it in partnership with my sisters and brothers in Christ.[30]

This promise describes the constitutional reality of the Episcopal Church. In a time when we are emphasizing the mutual exercise of ministry and the collaboration of all the baptized, it would be a healthy reminder to one and to all of the constitutional nature of the American episcopate.

In addition to the promise described above, the next revision might include a promise to be a leader in ministry and mission. The present examination speaks of the bishop encouraging and supporting all the baptized in their mission and ministry, but it does not explicitly speak of the bishop as one who leads the people in that mission and ministry. Here again the New Zealand ordinal stresses this leadership in mission and ministry at several points in "The Commitment."

Presiding Bishop Will you oversee with compassion and patience the people of God committed to your care? Will you give encouragement to all, and labour to strengthen the Church's witness and mission?

Bishop-elect I will. God give me grace to listen, grace to be fair and merciful, courage and boldness to proclaim the gospel.

Presiding Bishop Will you lead God's people in seeking the lost and lonely, in healing the sick and ministering to all, whatever their needs? Will you build up the Church in faith, and challenge us with the demands of love?

Bishop-elect I will. My concern will be to show love and compassion. God give me courage to strive for justice, wholeness and peace among all people.

Presiding Bishop As a bishop in the Church of God, will you help us to share in the life of the world-wide Christian community?

Bishop-elect Yes, I will. I will promote the unity and mission for which Christ prayed.[31]

These promises hold before the Church its mission and stress that this mission is given to the whole Church. By leading the Church in this, the bishops exercise one dimension of the ministry to which they have been called.

One dimension of the present examination should be expanded. In the 1979 ordinal, the rubric introducing the actual questions of the examination states that the questions are to be addressed to the bishop-elect "by one or more of the other bishops."[32] Since the bishop-elect is committing himself or herself to a ministry in collaboration with other bishops, presbyters, deacons, and laity, is it not desirable that the appropriate questions be asked by those who are directly affected? For example, could not the chair of the diocesan standing committee ask the bishop-elect whether he or she "[will]... boldly proclaim and interpret the Gospel of Christ, enlightening the minds and stirring up the conscience of your people"?[33] Could we not reorganize the lengthy question about episcopal collegiality, presbyteral collegiality, and care for the deacons and laity?[34]

Bishop Will you share with the bishops, clergy, and delegates of the General Convention in the government of the Episcopal Church?

Bishop-elect I will, with God's help.

Presbyter Will you sustain your fellow presbyters and take counsel with them in leading the Diocese?

Bishop-elect I will, with God's help.

Deacon Will you guide and strengthen the deacons and all others who minister in the Church?

Bishop-elect I will, for the sake of the servant Lord.

The bishop-elect is entering into the episcopal college. But he or she is also entering into a community of clergy and laity who have exercised their legitimate authority in electing him or her and who have been engaged in ministry together prior to that election. The commitment that the bishop-elect makes is to a broader community than just the House of Bishops, and this commitment should be symbolized by the involvement of that community in the promises made.

THE CONSECRATION OF THE BISHOP-ELECT

IN THE INTRODUCTION TO THE 1970 TRIAL USE ORDINAL, the revisers state that the ordination prayer is "the most solemn text of the ordination rite."[35] In that spirit, let us begin by looking more closely at the ordination prayer for a bishop in the present ordinal.

God and Father of our Lord Jesus Christ, Father of mercies and God of all comfort, dwelling on high but having regard for the lowly, knowing all things before they come to pass: We give you thanks that from the beginning you have gathered and prepared a people to be heirs of the covenant of Abraham, and have raised up prophets, kings, and priests, never leaving your temple untended. We praise you also that from the creation you have graciously accepted the ministry of those whom you have chosen.

The Presiding Bishop and other Bishops now lay their hands upon the head of the bishop-elect, and say together

Therefore, Father, make *N.* a bishop in your Church. Pour out upon *him* the power of your princely Spirit, whom you bestowed upon your beloved Son Jesus Christ, with whom he endowed the apostles, and by whom your Church is built up in every place, to the glory and unceasing praise of your Name.

The Presiding Bishop continues

To you, O Father, all hearts are open; fill, we pray, the heart of this your servant whom you have chosen to be a bishop in your Church, with such love of you and of all the people, that *he* may feed and tend the flock of Christ, and exercise without reproach the high priesthood to which you have called *him*, serving before you day and night in the ministry of reconciliation, declaring pardon in your Name, offering the holy gifts, and wisely overseeing the life and work of the Church. In all things may *he* present before you the acceptable offering of a pure, and gentle, and holy life; through Jesus Christ your Son, to whom, with you and the Holy Spirit, be honor and power and glory in the Church, now and forever.

The People in a loud voice respond Amen.[36]

As the prayer is presently constructed, it consists of three parts: (1) an opening address to the First Person of the Trinity, (2) the laying on of hands with a petition for the gift of the Holy Spirit for the office and work of a bishop, and (3) a concluding section of petitions for the grace of God to enable the new bishop to exercise her or his ministry faithfully and effectually.

The actual text of the prayer is "a rather free contemporary translation" of the ordination prayer for a bishop in the *Apostolic Tradition* of Hippolytus.[37] In stating their rationale for the choice of this prayer, the revisers indicate (1) that it is desirable to have a distinct prayer for each order and (2) that it has ecumenical significance, given the use of a translation of this prayer in the Roman Catholic rite for the ordination of a bishop.[38]

Without impugning the work of the previous revisers of the ordination rite, we may ask several questions about the continued use of this prayer in the ordination rites of the American Episcopal Church. First, does the language of the prayer speak to the experience of the Episcopal

Church as regards the ministry of bishops? Although our faith proclaims that God has raised us up to be heirs of the covenant made with Abraham and Sarah, we do not live in a world, nor have we for some time, in which bishops are expected to be akin to the monarchs of Israel and to the levitical priesthood. One does not deny to bishops the exercise of apostolic oversight by questioning whether the gift of the Holy Spirit in ordination is to be equated with the princely Spirit whom God bestowed upon the Beloved.

In good Anglican fashion, the decision to use a translation of the ordination prayer of Hippolytus was based upon historical, ecumenical, and theological grounds. What was not addressed as directly in this decision was the pastoral dimension, i.e., the reception of the text within a given community that lives in a given social and cultural context. The antiquity of a text does not justify its use. We must demonstrate how this text will give voice to our experience of the mystery it expresses. It must challenge us, not just to fidelity with an honored past, but to commitment to a faithful future. And it should call us to give the gospel we have received a North American Anglican skin.

Turning to the opening paragraph of the prayer, we note that the continued use of predominantly masculine language for God and for God's activity presents a problem for the American church at the end of the twentieth century. When the ordinal was being prepared in the late 1960s, inclusive language for God was not a major concern for liturgists, although efforts were made to reduce the use of masculine pronouns in other sections of the prayer book.[39] We have also noted the allusion to God's choosing of "prophets, priests, and kings" so that the Temple might never be unattended. This emphasizes a cultic dimension to the episcopate that, while not absent from a bishop's responsibilities, may not be the primary role of the episcopate in contemporary North American Anglicanism.

We may also examine more closely the assumptions made by the revisers in choosing the Hippolytan prayer. Is it necessarily desirable that distinct prayers be used for each office? At least one Anglican province has chosen to use an ordination prayer that is common to all three orders save only in the final paragraph. The opening paragraph of the New Zealand ordination prayer moves from God's creation of a people to the specific ministry being conferred.

Blessed are you, God our creator, God in history, God in revelation; throughout the ages your unchanging purpose has created a people to love and serve you.

Blessed are you in Christ Jesus, your Incarnation, our Servant Lord, who by death overcame death. Through resurrection and ascension, through the gift of the Holy Spirit, you have given life and order to your Church, that we may carry out the ministry of love. We thank you for calling this your servant to share this ministry as a (deacon, priest, bishop).[40]

Here we see an effort to focus primarily on God's purpose in calling forth a people to exercise mission and ministry rather than on a more narrow cultic dimension to episcopal ministry. This movement is also evident in the ordination prayer of the English and Canadian rites.

We praise and glorify you, almighty Father, because you have formed throughout the world a holy people for your own possession, a royal priesthood, a universal Church.

We praise and glorify you because you have given us your only Son Jesus Christ to be the Apostle and High Priest of our faith, and the Shepherd of our souls.

We praise and glorify you that by his death he has overcome death; and that, having ascended into heaven, he has given his gifts abundantly to your people, making some, apostles; some, prophets; some, evangelists; some, pastors and teachers; to equip them for the work of ministry and to build up his body.

And now we give you thanks that you have called this your servant, whom we consecrate in your name, to share this ministry entrusted to your Church.[41]

In both these examples we note an emphasis on the sharing by the ordained of the ministry given to the baptized.

When we turn to the actual petition for the gift of the Spirit, we encounter a significant area for revision. Our present ordination rites and the language of the ordination prayers tend to convey the impression that the rite confers to the person being ordained "something"not only the ordained, that he or she did not possess before the rite. The identity of this "something" is not always clear. Is it the authority to act publicly on behalf of the church? Is it some indelible character that represents an ontological change in the person being ordained? Is it the release of a charism to be used on behalf of the Church?

One major obstacle to answering this question is found in the language used at the time of the laying on of hands. The language suggests that the candidate is being given gifts that he or she did not possess prior to the ordination rite. Our ordination rites do not always reflect a theology of "giftedness," the conviction that the person being ordained has the charism for the office to which he or she is being ordained. Here I associate myself with Paul Gibson's thoughts as he writes about blessing in *Occasional Celebrations*, a liturgical publication of The Anglican Church of Canada.

> If we analyze our traditional Western forms of blessing we find that they tend to suggest that something has to be done to things like wedding rings and candlesticks and vestments and church buildings to make them fit for the holy purposes in which they are to be used.... The same point applies to the blessing of people. We bless people not to increase their spiritual dignity but to give thanks for the role they have been called to play within the reign of God and thus to release them to play their part. Every eucharistic prayer is such a blessing: we give thanks for the mighty acts of God and pray that those who gather at the table may be "one body and one holy people, a living sacrifice in Jesus Christ our Lord." Of course our traditional forms of blessing people may continue (e.g., "Almighty God... bless you"), but we should remember that they are prayers of thanksgiving for God's goodness and grace already received, and for its completion in these people.[42]

What would happen to the rite if we were to accept the premise that the bishop-elect already possesses the necessary gifts of the Spirit for office and that the ordination rite is an elaborate blessing, a rite that releases the bishop-elect's gifts to be used on behalf of the Church? Would we not perhaps want to ask something more like this: "God of grace, through your Holy Spirit, gentle as a dove, living, burning as fire, empower your servant N for the office and work of a bishop in the Church"?[43]

Finally, the New Zealand rite is unique in its conclusion to the ordination prayer in all three rites. After the petition for the empowerment of the Holy Spirit, the bishop in all three rites prays that the grace of ministry will rest on the ordinand, keeping him or her strong, faithful, and steadfast in Christ.[44] The final words, however, belong to the entire congregation.

> Amen! May *they* proclaim the good news, inspire our prayers, and show us Christ, the Servant. [from the prayer for deacons][45]

> Amen! May *they* herald the joy of your kingdom, bring freedom rather than bondage, serve rather than be served; through the sacraments *they minister* let your grace abound. [from the prayer for presbyters][46]

> Amen! May *s/he* point us to Christ, the Living Way, feed us with Christ, the Bread of Life, and unite us in Christ, rejoicing! [from the prayer for bishops][47]

With these petitions the entire assembly joins in the act of ordination in a concrete and appropriate fashion, affirming that the ordaining bishop or bishops do not act on their own authority alone but as presiders of the assembly. These petitions are analogous to our present practice at baptism when the congregation "confirms" the action of the presider: "We receive you into the household of God. Confess the faith of Christ crucified, proclaim his resurrection, and share with us in his eternal priesthood."[48]

CONCLUSION

IN THESE MUSINGS I HAVE SUGGESTED some of the revisions that I see as desirable in the ordination of a bishop. These revisions spring from the concern that our liturgical rites give clearer expression to the Good News of God in Jesus Christ as we North American Anglicans have received it and as we understand how this Good News is leading us in our mission and ministry.

Our experience is of a constitutional episcopacy that shares with the clergy and laity in the governance of the Church and in the discernment of how the truth of the gospel is to be expressed in the Church's doctrines. This experience requires that we make liturgical decisions that bring together the pastoral, theological, and historical dimensions of Christian faith. Pastoral decisions that ignore the apostolic preaching and the experience of two thousand years of Christian living risk rapid irrelevance. However, theological statements made in language not understood by the people may be true, but they cannot be lived authentically. Historical texts may be orthodox, but antiquity and orthodoxy do not guarantee that the text is *our* text, *our* prayer. Only by discovering the lively interplay of all three dimensions can we give voice to the gospel song that the Spirit has placed in our hearts.

Angels and Sheep Dogs:
The Role of Deacons in the Liturgy

Ormonde Plater

A FEW YEARS AGO, in a book about the diaconate, I wrote that deacons "continually explore their origins, try new directions, and test the limits of their ministry."[1] Today I see no reason to withdraw this observation. Despite resistance in some places to having deacons, in the last two decades deacons have become a lively presence and an important aspect of renewal in the Episcopal Church. This historic development has several origins: interest in the early Church, social needs in church and society, a desire for variety of leadership, and, above all, the movement of the Spirit in the Church. Much of the renewal of the diaconate can be traced to the ample provision for deacons in the 1979 *Book of Common Prayer*. If we take the prayer book seriously, we have to take deacons seriously, and we are moved to provide a place for them, both in liturgy and in the extended life of the Church.

Just as the Church locates the ministry of deacons in liturgy, the Church looks to liturgy for help in defining their meaning and elaborating their functions. In the eucharist, deacons read the gospel, lead the general intercessions, and prepare and serve the sacred meal. Thus deacons have a definitive leadership role in each of the three main parts of the eucharist: Word, prayer, and Sacrament.[2] Their role is symbolic as well as functional, and their iconography in the liturgy traditionally portrays angels—the messengers, heralds, warriors, and healing agents of God, swift and active in word and deed. It also suggests energetic and resourceful human beings such as ministers of state, staff officers, brokers, headwaiters, and butlers. From a another perspective, deacons are the sheep dogs of the Church, working among and around the herd.[3] Deacons do not preside; they prod and prompt.

Derived from liturgies of the third and fourth centuries, the eucharistic role of modern deacons reflects the finding of John F. Collins that ancient deacons were agents of the Church in word, action, and attendance, acting for and assisting the bishop in oversight.[4] They mirrored Christ, revealing Christ's role as *diakonos* or agent of God in Creation and salvation. Growing out of this agency, one of their primary ecclesial activities was not personal care of the needy, the *agape* duty of every Christian, but promotion and organization of corporate care, the *diakonia* duty of the Church. Such care was an essential ministry of the Church.

What deacons were in ancient times, they are today, not only in liturgy but in the broad life of the Church. As the 1995 Dublin statement describes them, "Deacons serve the church by marshalling, coordinating, and facilitating the various ministries of its members in the world. They should function in a similar way in the eucharistic assembly."[5] In prayer books before 1979, the ministry of deacons in the Episcopal Church was to become priests. Since 1979 the liturgy has expressed a far different ministry of deacons—particularly in the eucharist and the ordination rites—as a lifelong and serious commitment to a special leadership in the Church. Although this change in emphasis has been successful and a benefit to the Church, there is both a need and a desire for further changes in the liturgy. I suggest that these should have three main purposes: (1) to strengthen the ministry of deacons, (2) to portray them as members of a team, and (3) to remove or reduce their ministry as presiders. Anything done to clarify the meaning of deacons through reinforcement of their proper functions (and through suppression of functions inappropriate to deacons) will help all the ministries of the Church to become clearer and more useful.

For convenience, this discussion follows the sequence of the *Book of Common Prayer*, even though a future book, books, or even CD-ROM disks may take a different form. Many of my suggestions deal with rubrics, directions, and commentaries; some, with liturgical text.

CONCERNING THE SERVICE OF THE CHURCH

IN THIS INTRODUCTORY SECTION, deacons are described in negative terms as those who "do not exercise a presiding function." Paradoxically, the section goes on to provide several exceptions in which deacons may preside. Somewhere in a new prayer book, it would be better to characterize the ministers of the church as those who exercise symbolic roles with specific functions. After describing the presidential role of bishops and presbyters, the section might continue, "The role of deacons is not to preside but to function as messengers, agents, and attendants. Other baptized persons function in various leadership and serving roles, especially as readers of Scripture and leaders of song." I would resist specifying occasions when deacons may function as officiants and instead allow all baptized persons, without mentioning deacons, to preside in the Daily Office and certain other rites.

While reserving the authority of a bishop or priest to preside in the eucharist, the rubrics should allow "another baptized person" to preside in the following liturgies when a bishop or priest is not present: the Daily Office, Ash Wednesday, Good Friday, the Easter Vigil, and funerals.

A new prayer book also needs to be clearer about what "order" means. By referring to "the members of each order in the Church, lay persons, bishops, priests, and deacons," the present section implies that there are four orders. The preface to the ordination rites instead speaks of "three distinct orders." Are the baptized really ordained in baptism— or in confirmation, as some suppose? Or have we confused two different kinds of "order"—legislative (the clerical and lay orders) and ecclesiastical (the three orders)—in an attempt to advance the importance of baptism? Construing baptism as "ordination of the laity" denigrates baptism, which is surely more important than ordination in the lives of Christians and their identity as community. I question whether baptism in catholic tradition has ever been an ordination rite or ought to become one.

CALENDAR

TWO DEACONS NEED TO BE MOVED: Ephrem to June 9, his traditional date, and David Pendleton Oakerhater to August 31, the date of his death in 1931. Several deacons from the early church are prime candidates for the calendar: Olympias (410) on July 25, Radegund (587) on August 13, Phoebe of Cenchreae on September 3, Romanos the Melodist (ca. 540) on October 1, and Philip the Deacon on October 11. American candidates include William West Skiles (1862), a farmer and monk at Valle Crucis, North Carolina, on December 8.[6]

DAILY OFFICE

ANYONE MAY PRESIDE in the Daily Office. Why, then, make a distinction in the form of forgiveness between (bishops and) priests and the rest of us? This form is ambiguously either a prayer or a declaration, confusingly similar to sacramental absolution. It would be better to turn it into a pure prayer that any leader can say without distinction and that includes the presider in the plea for forgiveness. This observation applies also to the similar forms in "A Penitential Order" and "Ministration to the Sick."

A cathedral or popular office is an entirely different liturgy in which ministers function by order much as they do in the eucharist. The present "Order of Worship for the Evening" sometimes equates priests and deacons, sometimes distinguishes between them. Provision might be made for a complete cathedral office—morning, evening, and vigil—in which deacons chant litanies and dismissals (morning and evening), the thanksgiving for light (evening), and the gospel (vigil). The role of a deacon in the evening office, especially in the candle liturgy, is related to that in the Easter Vigil.

ASH WEDNESDAY

AS IN THE DAILY OFFICE, the form for forgiveness is ambiguous and quasi-sacramental. It would be better to allow "another baptized person" to say a recast prayer for God's forgiveness, kneeling. We need to decide whether this rite is a corporate sacramental confession, requiring a priest. A deacon might do the invitation to a holy Lent.

PALM SUNDAY

AT THE PASSION GOSPEL, the rubric appears to allow the omission of deacons. I would recast it to read, "Together with deacons, any baptized person may take part in the reading or chanting of the passion gospel."

GOOD FRIDAY

THE RUBRIC AT THE PASSION GOSPEL should be as on Palm Sunday, above.

The Solemn Collects might be renamed The Solemn Prayers, since collects are only part of these general intercessions. The rubric about posture needs to read, "The people may be directed to kneel during the silence and to stand for the collects." It would be helpful to print the deacon's direction: "Let us kneel in silent prayer" and "Arise."

In a week of many processions, there is a strong connection between bringing a wooden cross into church and entering with the Paschal Candle. The rubrics might provide for a fuller ceremony. A deacon carries the cross, singing three times at an even higher pitch, "Behold the wood of the cross, on which hung the savior of the world," and the people respond each time, "Come, let us worship."

THE GREAT VIGIL OF EASTER

ALTHOUGH THE OPENING DIRECTIONS allow a lay person to chant the Exsultet in the presence of a deacon, hearing a deacon is more important than hearing a melodious voice. The rubric should read, "In the absence of a deacon, another baptized person may chant the Exsultet." While strengthening deacons in diaconal functions, we should discourage them from presiding. In the absence of a priest or bishop, we should allow "another baptized person" to lead the liturgies of light, Word, and baptism and to administer communion from the reserved Sacrament.

The present Exsultet needs revision: changing "fathers" to "ancestors" and "man is" to "we are;" removing the doxology from the "Rejoice" part (which makes it seem a prayer instead of a command to all Creation); adding an optional "O happy fault" clause. Even better would be a new Exsultet—or two—and permission to use alternative texts or to create one. The standard texts might include those from the new Roman sacramentary and a version, perhaps metrical, in the language of modern poetry. A modern Exsultet should be a fresh translation with vivid imagery, as in this sample beginning:

Leap now, angel swarms of heaven,
twist and turn around God's throne,
blow your trumpets, shout salvation.
Christ our king in triumph reigns!

A revised or new Exsultet might also provide refrains for the people—for example, the first verse of *Phos hilaron* after each of the initial strophes; the paschal troparion "Christ is risen from the dead" between major sections of the candle blessing. If the people have a lively part, they won't mind that an unmusical deacon monotones or even croaks the text.

During the Liturgy of the Word, before each prayer a deacon might direct, "Let us stand in silent prayer."

HOLY BAPTISM

ADDRESSED TO GOD, the biddings in the prayers for the candidates are not specifically diaconal, although in some places deacons routinely lead them. The rubrics should specify "a sponsor or other baptized person." Following ancient practice, a deacon may perform the water baptism. It is far less appropriate for a deacon to preside over baptism with a congregation, as the additional directions permit. The scriptural precedent of Philip's baptism of the Ethiopian eunuch (Acts 8:26-40), supported by many later examples, suggests that deacons and other Christians may baptize in cases of emergency or unusual need. Aside from emergencies, a congregation can await the next visit of the bishop.

Perhaps a new prayer book will incorporate the catechumenate into a unified rite of Christian initiation. The liturgical role of deacons can be enhanced, drawing on their role as teachers of ministry to the learner Christians. Based on ancient practice, as described in *Apostolic Constitutions*, deacons should give the dismissal "Cathechumens, go in peace."

HOLY EUCHARIST

"CONCERNING THE CELEBRATION" SETS FORTH the functions of deacons and other ministers. In this section, we should recognize officially that deacons by ordination are the normal leaders of intercession. We should allow other baptized persons to share in that function, joining with but never displacing deacons, and we should give them a fuller role in serving at the table. All these activities, performed by deacons and others, liberate the presider to be more presidential and priestly. I suggest the following:

• It is the function of deacons to read the gospel, to lead the Prayers of the People, and to serve at the table. Deacons prepare and place on the table the bread and cup of wine and assist in distributing communion. In the absence of a deacon, a bishop or priest may read the gospel.

• Other baptized persons proclaim the readings that precede the gospel, and they may join in leading the Prayers of the People. In the absence of a deacon, they may lead the Prayers of the People, and they may prepare and place on the table the bread and wine. When authority is given by the bishop, they may assist in distributing communion.[7]

Here and elsewhere, the rubrics and text should provide for two or more deacons in the eucharist, without being specific about how they divide duties. (Having more than two is usually cumbersome, except in distributing communion.) The rubrics might, however, specify the functions of deacons when a bishop presides. If enough deacons are present, two attend the bishop and one or two others perform the normal duties of deacons in the eucharist.

At the Gospel, to enhance the solemnity of the proclamation, a new prayer book might provide for the deacon to greet the people with "The Lord be with you," as in the Canadian *Book of Alternative Services*. Alternatively, we might allow the deacon to proclaim a direction adapted from Orthodox liturgies: "Wisdom! Stand and hear the Good News of our Lord Jesus Christ." Then comes the Alleluia or other song and the announcement, "A reading from the Holy Gospel according to *N.*"

Although the custom of blessing the deacon before the Gospel has become widespread, presiders are not always sure what they should say or do. The book might provide two traditional forms: First (with the sign of the cross), "The Lord be in your heart and on your lips that you may worthily proclaim his Holy Gospel: In the name of the Father, and of the Son, and of the Holy Spirit;" second (with laying on of hands), "May the Spirit of the Lord be upon you as you bring Good News to the poor."

Many have complained about routine and unimaginative renderings of the Prayers of the People. The given forms are often unrelated to local needs and customs, and until recently few congregations took advantage of the subtle and ambiguous permission to change the forms or compose new ones. A new book should give clear directions, as does the Canadian *Book of Alternative Services*, for the leader and others to "use creativity and discretion" in planning the general intercessions, to modify and mold the prayers to those who pray them, and to provide scope for the worshippers to add their own names and concerns. With the proliferation of intercessions in books and even on the World Wide Web,[8] inspired by Scripture and current experience, I question whether we need forms in the prayer book. What we need is encouragement to write our own prayers and to use the many resources available elsewhere. Among the directions for intercession, the list of required topics might be reduced from six to four:

- the church and its mission
- the world and the created order
- the local community
- all in need (including the dead)[9]

To strengthen their intercessory character, I would omit from the Prayers of the People any provision for individual thanksgivings. A more appropriate place for thanksgivings is either just before the eucharistic prayer or just after communion (see below).

Before the Peace, especially following a confession of sin, a deacon might direct the people to stand, by word or gesture.

At the kiss of peace, many presiders invite the people to exchange a greeting, often turning the rubric into a liturgical sentence. After the presider's salutation "The peace of the Lord be always with you" and the people's response, a deacon might add, "Offer one another a sign of peace."

At the preparation of the gifts, a deacon performs four distinct actions, which might be expressed more cogently in a rubric such as the following:

A deacon normally prepares the table, receives the bread and wine, prepares them, and places them on the table. In the absence of a deacon, another baptized person may do this. Representatives of the people present the gifts of bread and wine for the eucharist (with money and other offerings) to the deacon or other person. The people stand while the gifts are presented and placed on the table. When the bread and wine are ready, the presider comes to the altar.

It is important to emphasize that deacons are ordained to prepare the table. Those who prepare the table in the absence of a deacon do so as a part of the people's offering of gifts, not as substitutes for deacons.

Just before the eucharistic prayer, a deacon might invite the people to offer their own thanksgivings: "As we prepare to give thanks over this bread and wine, let us give thanks for the many gifts of God." When they have finished, the presider begins. Another logical place for extempore thanksgivings is just before the postcommunion prayer.

If the introduction to a memorial acclamation is addressed to the people (rather than to God, as in the present eucharistic prayers), it would be appropriate for a deacon to say it, for example, "Let us proclaim the mystery of faith."

Rubrics might provide for an optional elevation of the bread by the presider and the cup of wine by a deacon, both at the doxology of the prayer and at the invitation to communion. These are two different gestures: the first offering, the second inviting.

If the breaking of the bread contains directions such as those in the *Book of Occasional Services*, they should include the instruction that "during the [fraction] anthem, deacons and others may bring additional vessels to the table and prepare them for communion."

The rubric about receiving communion should avoid mandating a hierarchical sequence and allow the presider and deacons to receive last, as already happens in some places: "The presider, the deacons and other ministers of the eucharist, and the people then receive communion."

After communion in many places, the eucharistic ministers take bread and wine for the communion of absent members. A revised book should recognize this action and name deacons as those who train, coordinate, and send these ministers on their mission.

Before solemn blessings, a deacon might direct the people: "Bow your heads for God's blessing." At the Dismissal, we might allow a deacon to dismiss the people "with these or similar words." There is no theological reason for reserving the Dismissal to the presider when a deacon is not present. Although we can easily allow "another baptized person" to dismiss, no one should displace a deacon from this function.

COMMUNION UNDER SPECIAL CIRCUMSTANCES

THE TITLE AND PURPOSES OF THIS LITURGY, widely used by deacons taking communion to the sick and shut-in, need to be stated more clearly. Ideally, it is "Extended Communion for Those Not Present at the Celebration," using the Sacrament reserved from the most recent Sunday or festal celebration. The communicants include absent members and others outside the celebration (prisoners, hospitalized people from out of town, and the like). The rite should be designed for all (including priests, deacons, and eucharistic ministers) who administer communion to those people and the only required parts should be a short reading, the Lord's Prayer, and giving communion.

ADDITIONAL DIRECTIONS

THE PROVISION FOR A DEACON to preside (up to the peace) in the absence of a priest truncates the eucharistic liturgy and misuses the order of deacons. A similar criticism should be made of the liturgy of the pre-sanctified led by a deacon (once called deacon's mass). In this the people are deprived of two essential actions (offering gifts of bread and wine and giving thanks over them), and the deacon is turned into an unordained priest. A liturgy of the pre-sanctified is appropriate when led by a bishop or priest on days such as Good Friday but unsuitable for normal use by a deacon. The solution is for the congregation to celebrate Morning Prayer or, better, for the Church to provide priests in every place. Let's get rid of the deacon's mass.[10]

MARRIAGE

THE TRUE FUNCTION OF DEACONS IN MARRIAGE is to assist the presider, and the prayer book properly allows them to deliver the charge and ask for the declaration of consent. The rubrics in the rite need to reflect this permission, saying before each of those sections, "the presider or a deacon." Less desirable is the permission for deacons to perform marriages when no bishop or priest is available. Those intending to marry have sufficient time either to find one or to wait for one.

The Prayers of the People need a simpler form, with biddings directed to the people and a strong response. There should also be permission to adapt another form or to compose one, so long as it emphasizes the community in which this holy relationship is a sign.

RECONCILIATION OF A PENITENT

THE DECLARATION OF FORGIVENESS to be used by a deacon or lay person is an ambiguous quasi-absolution and, I suspect, rarely used. It would be better to restrict the presidency of sacramental confession to a bishop or priest.

MINISTRATION TO THE SICK

EXCEPT WHEN THE "MINISTRATION TO THE SICK" includes the eucharist, there is no theological reason why any baptized person may not lead the entire service, including anointing and laying on hands. The rubric allowing deacons or lay persons to anoint "in cases of necessity" has caused confusion. What is a case of necessity? Presumably, it is any time a bishop or priest cannot be present, which includes almost all visits to the sick by deacons and others. Does the rubric allow anointing but prohibit laying on hands? Let's open the full sacramental action to all who visit as ministers of the Church.

MINISTRATION AT THE TIME OF DEATH

THE RITE NEEDS TO PROVIDE FOR the giving of last communion, or viaticum (food for a journey), after the Lord's Prayer or the prayer "Deliver your servant," with words such as these: "N., receive this food for your journey. The Body of Christ, the bread of heaven. The Blood of Christ, the cup of salvation."

BURIAL OF THE DEAD

UNLIKE MARRIAGE, DEATH AND BURIAL DO NOT ALWAYS have the luxury of waiting for an available priest. Deacons are no more appropriate than anyone else, and the rubric should specify "any baptized person" in the absence of a priest.

The Prayers of the People need simple forms, with biddings directed to the people and a strong response. There should also be permission to use or adapt another form or to compose one.

ORDINATION RITES

FROM WHAT WE KNOW about where the diaconate originated and where it appears to be going, the description in the preface is inadequate and limiting. It should say something like this:

Third, there are deacons who assist bishops and priests in all this work. Acting for the church, they function in ministries of liturgy, word, and charity, especially by mobilizing the church's ministry with the poor, the sick, the suffering, and the helpless.

Ordination to all three orders should include deacons among the presenters.

For a bishop, the directions might tell how to use several deacons: two to attend the chief consecrator, two to attend the new bishop after the consecration, at least one more as senior deacon for Gospel and table, and others as needed. A deacon should proclaim the Gospel, and deacons should "prepare the table, receive and prepare the elements, and place them on the table."

For a priest, the present rite presumes their absence. Instead, deacons should read the Gospel, serve at the table in the usual way, and dismiss the people.

ORDINATION OF A DEACON

THE PRESENCE OF OTHER DEACONS should always be assumed, and the rubrics should clearly direct them to perform their normal functions.

The present rite assumes the ordination of only one deacon. Instead, in many dioceses the bishop ordains deacons in groups. Whether ordaining one or several, the rubrics and text can reflect the plurality and collegiality of deacons in several ways. Revisers should consider whether to have others join the bishop in laying on hands — all the deacons (as in Armenian tradition) or even everyone present. If either of these seems too innovative or impractical, the deacons present can at least form a semicircle around the bishop and ordinands. In some dioceses, the examination of the ordinands provides an occasion for all the deacons present to renew their ordination vows. In a few dioceses, diaconal ordinations take place within a celebration of the total ministry of the congregation, including presbyteral ordinations and the appointment of other ministers, requiring extensive adjustments in the rite.

The essence of ordination is election to office, prayer, and laying on of hands, and each of these elements needs to receive emphasis in a simplified rite. A deacon should lead the litany for ordinations, which could be simpler and reflect leadership in the midst of community rather than over it. The examination of the ordinand has often been quoted in sermons and articles, usually as a source of the meaning and functions of deacons. Instead, it is an insertion, a commentary placed within the liturgy.[11] Some of its material should be incorporated into the ordination prayer. Some of the examination repeats promises already made in the

Baptismal Covenant, reaffirmed at each baptism, and I wonder why new deacons have to rehearse them as a condition of ordination.

The prayer of consecration also raises problems. The use of "servant" as a translation of *doulos* in allusions to Phil. 2:7 and Mark 10:44 suggests that we are ordaining slaves. A heavy reliance on "servant" language tends to restrict our understanding of the great diversity and scope of deacons.[12] We need a new prayer, combing ancient and modern sources and responsive to the directions the diaconate has been taking and is likely to take. As a possible prayer, I have drafted the following:

Blessed are you,
God and Father of our Lord Jesus Christ.
You speak, and all things stir in being.
You breathe, and all things move in order.
Your Word speeds forth
to serve your will,
to show your desires,
to reveal your love,
and all things sing your praise.
Glory to you forever.

Now send your Spirit on this assembly,
shine your face on these servants of God,
chosen deacon in the Church,
and fill them with grace and power.
Glory to you forever.

Make them modest and humble,
strong and constant,
swift and active,
as they carry out your will
among your holy people.
Give them your Spirit
as they bring Good News to the poor,
lead our prayers for all in need,
and serve your banquet
in the gathered Body of Risen Christ.
Glory to you forever.

All glory and honor to you
through Jesus Christ your Servant,
with the Holy Spirit in the Holy Church,
now and to the ages of ages. *Amen.*[13]

As the Word-Christ acts for God, deacons act for the Body of Christ. The present method of laying on hands interrupts and divides the prayer. Rubrics might direct:

If only one deacon is being ordained, the bishop lays hands on this person during the entire prayer.

If two deacons are being ordained, the bishop lays a hand on each of them during the entire prayer.

If more than two deacons are being ordained, the bishop first lays hands on each of them, in silence, and then extends hands over all of them during the entire prayer.

Such a direction restores the ancient practice connecting this action with the entire prayer, while retaining personal contact when there are several deacons. It also avoids the suggestion of a moment of consecration during the epiclesis. Like eucharistic prayers, the entire prayer is consecratory, and there is no need to repeat parts of it for each deacon.[14]

The present rubric about vesting with "other insignia of the office of deacon" is imprecise. I would specify that members of the congregation vest each deacon with two distinctive garments: "dalmatic and stole over the left shoulder." If an instrument is to be conferred, let us give the Book of Gospels or other liturgical book and not a personal Bible (a better gift at baptism).

The ordination of a deacon in transit to the priesthood presents a peculiar problem. All present are required to subscribe to the polite fiction that the person has been truly called "to the life and work of a deacon." The solution is to get rid of the transitional diaconate. But until that moment arrives, we should alter the text in at least two places. The presenters might present the ordinand "to be ordained a deacon in Christ's holy catholic church, in preparation for ordination to the priesthood."[15] In the examination the bishop might ask, "Do you believe that you are truly called by God and his Church to the life and work of a priest, after time as a deacon?"

CELEBRATION OF A NEW MINISTRY

MANY HAVE TRIED to adapt this clericalized and often criticized liturgy for the installation of deacons. Rather than have a special liturgy, the deacon might perform as normal in the eucharistic liturgy. At the end, the deacon would be welcomed in the announcements, greeted by all, and immediately dismiss the people. Applause for a job well done is more sincere than a lot of extravagant expectations.

As the Catechism points out, all Christian ministers represent Christ and his Church. In the three orders, this representation has a distinct focus and meaning, located within the Church and existing for the good of the Church. Empowered by the Spirit, bishops and presbyters act in the person of Christ the head of the Body; deacons, in the person of Christ the *diakonos* of God. Bishops represent Christ as teacher, presider, and high priest. Sharing in this governing role, presbyters represent Christ as builder and local leader of the Body. Assisting in their leadership of the assembly, deacons represent Christ as servant, agents directed by the bishop. In particular, today, bishops direct deacons to lead baptized persons in ministries of mercy, justice, and peace. Because all three act in the person of Christ, they act in the person of the Church. We should remember that the ministry of the Church, despite all its variety and differences, is the one ministry of Christ. Through all the ministries of the Church, we express this truth in our great work for the People of God, the sacred liturgy.

Leaping Beyond
the Bonds of Boundaries

A Truly Common Prayer:
An Anglican-Lutheran Prayer Book

Philip H. Pfatteicher

THE EMERGING ANGLICAN AND LUTHERAN MOVEMENTS maintained close contacts during the first half of the sixteenth century. The direction of influence at that time was generally from the continent to England. At Cambridge, future leaders of the Church of England studied Luther's writings; Luther's work influenced the Bible translations of William Tyndale and Miles Coverdale (1535). In 1536 a dialogue between Anglican and Lutheran theologians (including Robert Barnes, Martin Luther, and Philipp Melanchthon) took place in Wittenberg and resulted in the "Wittenberg Articles," which, together with other dialogues such as the Württemberg Conference of 1552, influenced a series of Anglican articles up to the Thirty-nine Articles of Religion (1571).

Luther began his liturgical work in 1523 with three works: his essay "Concerning the Ordering of Divine Worship in the Congregation," his baptismal order, and his reformation of the Mass, *Formula Missae*. A quarter of a century later (1549), the Church of England had its *Book of Common Prayer*. Lutheran influence on that first prayer book was significant.

> Archbishop Cramer... was intimately acquainted with the Lutheran Service, having spent a year and a half in Germany in conference with theologians and princes, and he was most intimate with Osiander when he was at work on the Brandenburg-Nürnberg Order, in 1532. Two Lutheran Professors were called to English Universities, and aided in this work, one of whom, Bucer, had with Melanchthon and others prepared the Revised Order of Cologne, 1543. And... during the years from 1535 to 1549, there had been constantly recurring embassies and conferences between the Anglican and Lutheran divines and rulers.[1]

The construction of Morning Prayer from pre-Reformation Matins and Lauds and of Evening Prayer from Vespers and Compline had been anticipated by Luther's suggestions, by church orders of Bugenhagen, and by the Calenberg and Göttingen Order of 1542. The English litany incorporated petitions and extensive phrases of Luther's revision of the Litany of the Saints (1529) as found in the Reformation of Archbishop Hermann of Cologne (1543). In the Holy Communion, the use of entire psalms instead of the historic Introits may be traced to Luther's suggestion in his Formula Missae: "We approve and retain the introits for the Lord's days and for the festivals of Christ... although we prefer the Psalms from which they were taken as of old."[2] But his suggestion was generally not followed by Lutheran church orders. Expressions in the exhortations, the Confession and Absolution, the Prayer for the Whole State of Christ's Church, the beginning of the Prayer of Consecration, and the second half of the Benediction are from Hermann's Reformation of Cologne. The Verba area provides a harmony of New Testament accounts as in the Brandenburg-Nürnberg church order (1533).[3] The orders for baptism and marriage conform in structure and details to suggestions by Luther and Bucer. The 1549 *Book of Common Prayer* thus made a considerable use of Lutheran precedents well established in Germany and Scandinavia.

For a variety of reasons (cultural, intellectual, and political), these early relationships gave way to separate theological and ecclesiastical developments during the next two centuries and to mutual isolation and to the resulting ignorance and misrepresentation. Anglicans and Lutherans often had little to do with each other.

There were exceptions. At Gloria Dei Church in Philadelphia, the Swedish Lutherans who had founded the parish in 1677 encountered difficulty in getting the Church of Sweden to supply priests. The German Lutherans, who were predominant in Pennsylvania, seemed quite foreign in language and policy. So the Swedish Americans, who were using English, turned rather naturally to the church they saw in the United States that seemed most like the Church of Sweden with its bishops and liturgy and vestment: Gloria Dei accepted Episcopal priests and the *Book of Common Prayer*. In 1845 Gloria Dei became a parish of the Episcopal Diocese of Pennsylvania. The other Swedish congregations in Philadelphia and surrounding areas followed a similar course and became Episcopal parishes.

In the nineteenth century Lutherans and Anglicans began recovering their long-ignored theological and liturgical heritage. In that century, as in the sixteenth, theological recovery came first, and it led naturally to liturgical restoration and renewal. In its reclamation of the Catholic tradition, the Oxford movement developed a distinctly anti-Reformation spirit, but the original relationships and influences were not forgotten, at least from the Lutheran side.

When Lutherans began to use English in worship, two centuries after the first prayer books, the earlier direction of influence was reversed. This time it was the Lutherans' turn to make use of the experience and work of the Anglicans. Lutherans in London in the eighteenth century used the prayer book orders for baptism and marriage for their English services. These were incorporated in the German manuscript liturgies used in America by Lutheran pastors in Henry Melchior Muhlenberg's time. (Muhlenberg's own son William Augustus [1796-1877] was to become an Episcopal priest in part because he wanted to use English in worship; he is commemorated on the Episcopal calendar on April 8.) Lutherans in Nova Scotia in 1864, "feeling the necessity of having a liturgy of our church suitable for a British congregation," prepared an abbreviated edition of the prayer book for their own use and published it as *The Book of Common Prayer* and *Administration of the Sacraments...according to the Use of the Lutheran Church in Nova Scotia*. In the United States, English-speaking Lutherans incorporated in their emerging common service the prayer book translation of the collects and other liturgical texts, such as the Lord's Prayer, the Creeds, Gloria in excelsis, the Preface, Te Deum. The Lutherans who were learning to use English in worship turned naturally to the church most like themselves, which had a long acquaintance with English and freely borrowed prayer book language and translations. Moreover, material original to the Lutheran books was "cast in forms of expression fixed for all English-speaking people in the Prayer Books of the sixteenth century."[1] The translation of the Gregorian collect for the first Sunday in Advent, for example, sounds as if it came from the prayer book, but in fact it did not. It was translated by the Lutheran liturgists in 1868 who had learned well how to speak and pray in the classic English style.

Stir up, we beseech thee, thy power, O Lord, and come; that by thy protection we may be rescued from the threatening perils of our sins, and saved by thy mighty deliverance; who livest and reignest with the Father and the Holy Ghost, ever one God, world without end.

That tradition of language and style was, they recognized, nothing foreign. The Preface to the Common Service (1888) observed:

The Lutheran Revision of the Communion Service had been issued in many editions, for use in many States and cities, had been fully tested by more than twenty years of continuous use, and had even, at Luther's instigation, been provided with complete music, varied for all the Festivals, for full Choral Service, and issued in a superb volume, before the revision of the old Service was made by the Anglican Church and issued in the First Prayer Book of Edward VI.

There is an extremely close agreement between this First Prayer Book of the Church of England and the Common Service... It is therefore not at all strange that the first and best Service Book of the Church of England should have so closely followed the Lutheran use as to present very few divergencies from it. And should that church and her daughters return to the Use of the Book of Edward VI, as many of her most learned and devout members have ever wished, there would be an almost entire harmony in the Services of worship between the two daughters of the Reformation, who both have purified and then have preserved the Services of the Christian Church of the olden time.[5]

The Lutheran liturgists were clearly proud of the influence exerted by their theology and by "the pure Lutheran Liturgies of the Sixteenth Century."

The ecumenical movement of the twentieth century fostered new encounters between Anglicans and Lutherans. In 1908 the Lambeth Conference initiated conversations between the Church of England and the Lutheran Churches of Sweden (since 1908/1909) and Finland, Latvia, Estonia, Norway, Denmark, and Iceland (since 1930). These conversations led to several agreements concerning eucharistic sharing hospitality.[6]

After World War II, contacts between Anglicans and Lutherans on many levels led to increased mutual knowledge and recognition of the heritage they shared. The outstanding result of these conversations so far has been the Porvoo Common Statement of 1992 between four Anglican churches (the Church of England, the Church of Ireland, the Scottish Episcopal Church, and the Church in Wales) and eight Lutheran churches in northern Europe (Denmark, Finland, Iceland, Norway, Sweden, Estonia, Latvia, and Lithuania). After only four plenary sessions between 1989 and 1992, the representatives of these churches affirmed the significance of the episcopate in historic succession as sign and service of apostolic continuity and catholic unity of the whole Church.[7] This crucial agreement allows a recognition of existing ministries, and mutual participation in the consecration of bishops as an expression of existing communion.

In 1988 the Church of England and the Lutheran, United and Reformed churches in Germany concluded the Meissen Agreement on eucharistic sharing and closer relationships.[8] Since 1994 the Church of England and the Lutheran and Reformed churches in France have begun a round of conversations. In Africa there have been consultations between Anglican and Lutheran bishops; in Africa and in Asia, occasional mutual participation in the consecration of bishops.[9]

In the United States, Episcopalians and Lutherans have been in dialogue since 1969. The first report, published in 1973, did not result in action by the sponsoring churches, but the churches did authorize another round of dialogues. The second series met between 1976 and 1981. (It was during these years that the new prayer books were introduced, the *Lutheran Book of Worship* in 1978 and the *Book of Common Prayer* in 1979.) This second series of Episcopal-Lutheran dialogues resulted in the affirmation by the participating churches in their commitment to the goal of full communion, the establishment of an interim sharing of the eucharist, and the authorization of a third round of dialogues to discuss any outstanding issues on the way to full communion. These goals were set forth in the Lutheran-Episcopal Agreement of

1982. The third series of dialogues took place between 1983 and 1991 and issued two reports: one on the implications of the gospel (1989), and another on intercommunion with a Concordat of Agreement (1991). A Lutheran-Episcopal Joint Coordinating Committee was established by the Episcopal Church and the Evangelical Lutheran Church in America to implement the 1982 agreement. A time line was established with the approval of the sponsoring churches, and the two churches are to take action on the recommendations from the last series of dialogues at their national conventions in 1997.

Thus in many ways and throughout the world, Anglicans and Lutherans are growing closer together and recovering a relationship that was in existence at the Reformation. Whatever the fate of the Concordat, Lutherans and Anglicans must soon come to understand that much of what seemed in the past to require us to be distinct and unique no longer obtains. Conversations and sharing must lead to practical considerations. And the practical task that is the concern of the present collection of essays is the revision of the prayer book. Worldwide relationships, and specifically the proposed intercommunion between the Episcopal Church and the Evangelical Lutheran Church in America, suggest that we cooperate and work together on the revision of our prayer books.

The pattern laid down in the sixteenth and in the nineteenth centuries still applies at the dawn of the twenty-first century: Theological agreement issues naturally and necessarily in liturgical cooperation.

The mergers of Lutherans in North America are now realistically complete. The Lutheran Church-Missouri Synod (and its counterpart the Lutheran Church-Canada), an instrumental part of the creation of the Lutheran Book of Worship until the very end, is not likely to be open to join with other Lutherans in the foreseeable future. Indeed, it is generally agreed that the real reason for the last-minute withdrawal of the Lutheran Church-Missouri Synod from the endorsement and publication of the *Lutheran Book of Worship* was the fear of the obvious question in the face of the publication of the book: "If we use the same book, why shouldn't we be one organization?" (There was, of course, a "blue ribbon committee" that found the book unacceptable on theological grounds. But these findings came as a surprise to the Missouri Synod members of the several committees who had themselves never evidenced such concerns and who had indeed contributed greatly to the work that was finally to be rejected by their church. And it was the Missouri Synod that in the first place had issued the invitation to cooperate in work on one book.) There is no further Lutheran merger likely on this continent in the next generation. The Episcopalians in the United States have for a few decades now begun to act like Lutherans: splintering and fragmenting for allegedly doctrinal reasons, each dissident group declaring that it is more orthodox than everyone else. The prospect of putting American Anglicans back together does not seem to this observer to be a realistic possibility for this generation.

There is, however, a most promising and exciting ecumenical action before both churches: the proposed concordat between the Episcopal Church and the Evangelical Lutheran Church in America. Our present "interim" intercommunion, as well as the hope of the approval of the concordat by both churches, impels me to say what I have written and spoken before: It is devoutly to be hoped that the *Lutheran Book of Worship* is the last exclusively Lutheran service book published on this continent.[10] To Episcopalians I would respectfully suggest that the 1979 *Book of Common Prayer* be the last exclusively Episcopal prayer book in America. Lutherans and Episcopalians from now on should be in a relationship of growing confidence and trust that will enable them to share one book.

One of the useful pleasures of working on the preparation of the *Lutheran Book of Worship* (1978) was watching the parallel work on the drafting of the 1979 *Book of Common Prayer*. In fact, we who served on the various drafting committees were able, not only to watch what the Episcopalians were doing, but to benefit from solutions we saw in Episcopal books and to borrow from them not infrequently, even incorporating into the Lutheran book whole compositions from the prayer book.[11] The most notable and extensive borrowing is the entire Psalter, adopted with just one change. Psalm 8 in the Lutheran book begins "O LORD, our Lord"; Lutherans had used the Authorized (King James) Version in previous books, and "Governor" was not familiar in this context. We chose the prayer book Psalter because if the Anglicans' long experience with prayer in English and with singing the Office. In addition to the Psalter, the texts of the Lutheran book and of the prayer book throughout are notably similar and often identical, for we had traveled parallel tracks.

This borrowing is no innovation. The title of the 1888 Common Service deliberately reflected the Common Prayer of the Anglican communion, and the title *Common Service Book* more clearly echoed the title of the *Book of Common Prayer*. The 1888 Preface, quoted above, recognized the influence of Lutheran theology and liturgical revision on the 1549 prayer book. When Lutherans began to use English in worship, their books consciously used prayer book language and forms.

Now Episcopalians and Lutherans begin to look toward the revisions of their books, however distant that publication may be (and may that day be far hence).[12] The time has come to consider the next step in cooperation. Instead of working in tandem, as we have before, this time we must work together. More that, we must work together on one prayer book to serve both churches. Such a project is not as strange a suggestion as it may at first seem. The *Book of Common Prayer* and the *Lutheran Book of Worship* differ in appearance, but their contents are virtually the same. This is no new phenomenon. The contents of the predecessor books were virtually identical also.

My original hope,[13] and still the ideal, was that a number of denominations could cooperate in the production of the next book: Anglicans, Lutherans, Presbyterians, Methodists, maybe the United Church of Christ and the Moravians. But such a project would entail a very great number of representatives who have never worked together before, who would not proceed on the basis of many shared assumptions. They would, realistically, issue (if any) not one but a central outline of eucharistic order with a number of denominational variants and options. That still may not be a bad idea. The Lutheran Common Service of 1888 was such a text, but it was based on a consensus of sixteenth-century German church orders and allowed for a certain diversity within the unity of the Western Catholic and Lutheran heritage.

The cooperation of just two churches with a long history of similar prayer books would be a workable and productive enterprise. The Episcopal Church and the Lutheran Church since the Reformation have employed the same services: Holy Communion, Morning Prayer (Matins), Evening Prayer (Vespers), the same lectionary, the same course of collects, the Great Litany. Our church buildings look very much alike.

Our ministers dress very much the same way (the Lutherans being generally slower to adopt the surplice—in the 1930s—and slower to recover the use of eucharistic vestments, although they are no longer uncommon). The ancient association of the Lord's Day with the Lord's Supper is increasingly apparent in our churches, as are processions led by a cross and sometimes candles and the use of the sign of the cross. We have a great deal in common already. We look and act a good bit alike on Sunday morning.

More important is our theological convergence. The Concordat of Agreement is the clearest evidence of our bilateral interest in cooperation and the interchangeability of clergy that stops just short of organic union.

A Lutheran pastor, seeing the 1976 *Draft Proposed Book of Common Prayer*, exclaimed to me, "Why don't we just adopt this!" He was being at least half serious. An answer to his question might well be, "In effect, we have." We Lutherans took the Psalter, the daily lectionary, a good bit of the eucharistic lectionary, most of the prayers and thanksgiving, and phrases and whole passages from every service in the prayer book.

Episcopalians need to be aware that the whole Lutheran liturgy is not contained in the familiar green pew edition of the *Lutheran Book of Worship*, the edition that contains the hymnal; the whole liturgy is contained in the Ministers Edition, supplemented by our *Occasional Services* (1982). If one examines the 1979 *Book of Common Prayer* and the Ministers Edition side by side, we can see that everything in the prayer book has a corresponding passage in the Lutheran books. The following tabulation of the contents of the prayer book with the pages in the Ministers Edition will make the correspondence clear.

Book of Common Prayer		*Lutheran Book of Worship,* *Ministers Edition*
Calendar		pp. 13-14, 40-45
Daily Office		
Morning Prayer		pp. 14-15, 46-57
Evening Prayer		pp. 16-17, 58-70
Compline		pp. 17, 71-78
Daily Devotion for Families	=	Responsive Prayer
		pp. 17, 79-85

(continued)

Book of Common Prayer	Lutheran Book of Worship, Ministers Edition
The Great Litany	pp. 17-18, 86-91
Collects	pp. 18-20, 121-91
Proper Liturgies for Special Days	
Ash Wednesday	pp. 21-22, 129-31
Sunday of the Passion	pp.22, 134-35
Maundy Thursday	pp. 22-23, 137-38
Good Friday	pp. 23-24, 139-43
Holy Saturday	———
The Great Vigil of Easter	pp. 24-25, 143-53
Holy Baptism	pp. 30-32, 188-89, 308-312
Holy Eucharist	pp. 25-29, 195-307
Pastoral Offices	
Confirmation and Reaffirmation	pp. 35-36, 324-47
Marriage	pp. 36-37, 189-90, 328-30
Thanksgiving for a Child	Occasional Services pp. 54-55
Reconciliation of a Penitent	pp. 34-35, 322-23
Ministration to the Sick	
Ministry of the Word	Occasional Services pp. 48-75
Laying on Hands & Anointing	Occasional Services pp. 99-102
Holy Communion	Occasional Services pp. 76-88
Prayers	Occasional Services pp. 48-75
Ministration at Time of Death	Occasional Services pp. 103-112
Burial	pp. 37-38, 190-91, 331-39
Episcopal Services	
ordination	Occasional Services
of a Bishop	pp. 218-23
of a Priest	pp. 192-203
of a Deacon	pp. 210-17

(continued)

Book of Common Prayer	Lutheran Book of Worship, Ministers Edition
Celebration of a New Ministry	Occasional Services pp. 224-34
Celebration of a Church	Occasional Services pp. 166-72
The Psalter	pp. 18-20, 340-440
Prayers and Thanksgiving	pp. 25, 105-117
The Catechism	[Small Catechism]
Historical Documents of the Church	[Book of Concord]
Athanasian Creed	pp. 25, 118-20
Tables for Finding Holy Days	———
Lectionary	
three-year	pp. 21, 121-91
daily office	pp. 18, 96-104

Virtually everything in the *Book of Common Prayer* has its close parallel in the Lutheran liturgy.

It is, in fact, simpler and easier to list the items that are different:

1. The prayer book includes propers for a service on Holy Saturday during the day; the Lutheran book does not, although the previous Lutheran book (*Service Book and Hymnal*, 1958) included the Epistle and Gospel for Holy Saturday appointed in the prayer book.

2. The prayer book includes the Tables for Finding Days; the present Lutheran book unfortunately does not provide these tables, although previous books included them.

3. The prayer book Catechism corresponds to Luther's *Small Catechism*, beloved of his followers, a book not infrequently included in Lutheran service books,[14] although not in the present book.

4. Likewise, the Historical Documents of the Church correspond to the collection of Lutheran Confessions, the *Book of Concord*,[15] a volume far too large (except for the three ecumenical creeds) to be included in a service book.

5. The Lutheran book does not include the Daily Office lectionary for Holy Days (because, when these days are observed in Lutheran parishes, it is more often with the eucharist than the Office).

The *Lutheran Book of Worship* includes a few items not found in the prayer book:

1. Seasonal propers are included for the Daily Office—invitatories, versicles for the service of light in Evening Prayer, psalm antiphons, antiphons to the Benedictus and Magnificat;

2. Also included is a service called Corporate Confession and Forgiveness for use in times of strife in the congregation or the community. The service is an expansion of the earlier Order for Public Confession that was previously used to prepare for the celebration of the Holy Communion a few days before the celebration.

3. In addition to the prayer book Psalter, the Lutheran book—like the Roman Catholic Liturgy of the Hours in which it is deeply dependent—includes a psalm prayer for each of the 150 psalms for use in the Daily Office.

4. In addition to the three-year lectionary, the Lutheran book, yielding to conservative concerns, includes a revision of the historic one-year lectionary, a lectionary that in actual practice, so far as I know, is no longer used anywhere.

5. The eucharistic propers, in addition to the collect and readings and psalm and preface, include alleluia verses and offertories and a notation of the proper liturgical color.

6. Finally, in an effort to avoid ante-communion and to avoid distorting Morning Prayer into a service with sermon and offering, the Lutheran book introduced a newly-created Service of the Word, a preaching service for use when the eucharist is not celebrated.

Of these differences, the first and fourth reflect the basic difference between the *Book of Common Prayer* and Lutheran liturgies: Cranmer removed choir elements and focused on texts; Luther and his followers found it nearly impossible to conceive of worship without music.

The *Lutheran Book of Worship* is the work of American and Canadian Lutherans working together. Working on a book for two countries with their sometimes subtle differences was most useful. Americans had to learn and be reminded that Canada is not the northernmost state of the United States but a proud nation with separate traditions, cultures, ways of speaking—a bilingual country, party of the British Commonwealth, whose sovereign is Queen Elizabeth. To take but one example, an American suggested that, instead of the churchy term *purificator*, the ordinary word *napkin* be used. The Canadians were mystified, for to them a napkin was a diaper, a "nappie." Asked what the would call a napkin, they replied, "serviette." It was the Americans' turn to be mystified. *Purificator* remained. Cooperative work that requires broadening one's horizons, opening to different assumptions, understanding one's own peculiarities in an eminently worthwhile enterprise.

Now the Canadian Church and the American church are two entirely separate bodies, the Canadians no longer simply a "section" of the American church. Both churches use the *Lutheran Book of Worship*, but both have begun to produce separate supplementary materials. Thus the Episcopal Church in the United States of America and the Evangelical Lutheran Church in America are wholly American church bodies. There is no longer the complication of one body being of international composition.

Moreover, Episcopalians and Lutherans share the same crises. Again and again, while talking with Episcopal colleagues and friends, I hear them say, "The problem in the Episcopal Church is... [theological drift, disregard for liturgical forms, gender extremism, a loss of the sense of the transcendent, uncertainty as to the role of bishops, etc.]," and I reply that such comments also describe the Lutheran church in this country. In both churches we have a great "common tradition which is the mother of us all—the magnus consensus of the Fathers and the Councils of the undivided church of the first millennium." We who would be faithful to that tradition must struggle against the rush to cultural accommodation, the captivity and devotion to the idols of this age, we must resist those who wish to re-make God and Christ and salvation in their own image, who wish to prune away the branches of tradition into a caricature of the richness of the gospel—as if it simply was "God loves you and gives you what you want."[16] Both Lutherans and Episcopalians are in serious crisis, struggling for our very lives as authentic catholic churches.

This crisis is not the reason for our cooperation, but it gives urgency to the task of working on a common prayer book. Both churches need all the help they can get in the struggle to keep faith with the past while moving into the uncertain future.

In Lutheran history in North America the preparation of a new service book has been preparatory to a merger of the cooperating bodies. The *Common Service Book* of 1917 led to the creation in 1918 of the United

Lutheran Church in America, merging the General Council, the General Synod, and the General Synod South, three bodies which in 1888 had produced the Common Service. The *Service Book and Hymnal* of 1958 resulted in the formation in 1960 of the American Lutheran Church in America. The *Lutheran Book of Worship* of 1978 led to the creation of the Evangelical Lutheran Church in America and the Evangelical Lutheran Church in Canada. The cooperating churches, by working together on a service book, came to understand and to trust each other and so were prepared for the union of their bodies. The joint liturgical work was a primary cause and facilitation of the eventual union of the churches. Having one book of worship led inevitably, and soon afterward, to the formation of one church.

As two families get to know each other, they need to accept the oddities of the other and acknowledge the peculiarities and embarrassments of themselves.[17] Certain Lutheran peculiarities would need to be taken into account in work on a common prayer book. As one example, some in the Lutheranism still insist that the Verba not be used within a prayer of thanksgiving. Most other denominations are overcoming this reformation peculiarity; it persists more strongly in certain Lutheran circles than elsewhere. The present Lutheran book, in an effort to meet such objections, provides three options: a traditional eucharistic prayer, a prayer of thanksgiving followed by the Verba (employing a now obsolete Swedish practice), and the Verba alone (following Luther's Latin Mass and his German Mass.) Note, however, that the supplementary volume *With One Voice* (1995) employs only complete eucharistic prayers and makes provision for nothing else. The eucharistic prayer seems clearly to be the way of the future for Lutheran liturgies. As another example, Lutherans expect the liturgy to be set to music and the liturgy and the hymnal to be bound together in one book for the convenience of the congregation.

On the Anglican side is the desire on the part of some to retain the use of "traditional" language, the classic language of prayer in English since the Reformation.

What would have been perhaps divisive was the practice in previous prayer books of inserting the confession in the middle of the eucharist. Lutherans, following medieval Roman tradition, expect the confession at the outset of the Mass. In a preparatory booklet for trial use,

Contemporary Worship 2: Holy Communion (1970), we tried putting confession in the middle of the service between the Creed and the intercessions, but the practice was roundly rejected. The 1979 prayer book, however, provides the option of confession at the beginning or in the middle before the Peace. The location of confession is therefore no longer divisive.

It is the ordinal that will require the most careful and profound work. Lutherans, frankly, have no clear idea what the ministry of the Church is (or have many varying ideas about it); I have heard Episcopalians say the same thing about their church. The ordination rite was included in previous Lutheran books; it was excluded from the present book because of the order was not yet completed in 1978 when the *Lutheran Book of Worship* was published.

The nature and necessity of confirmation remains a question for us all—Roman Catholics, Anglicans, Lutherans. Work on a common understanding could benefit us all.

The calendar of saints will present some not insurmountable problems. Each church has and will want to retain representatives of its own peculiar tradition in the United States and in Europe and elsewhere, and that is as it should be. A common calendar noting which of the commemorations are peculiar to Lutheran practice or Episcopal practice could enrich the understanding of the size and scope of the Church and thus enrich us all.[18]

Should the hymnal eventually come to be part of our common work, the benefit would be enormous. Episcopalians and Lutherans once shared a love for English hymnody and could sing the same hymn texts, usually to the same tunes. Now with the publication of the *Lutheran Book of Worship* and the *Hymnal 1982*, to say nothing of the spate of other denominational hymnals, we have each gone our separate ways in the revision and adaptation of the old language. What seemed quite intolerable to one, seemed quite acceptable to another. There seems to be little logic to the choices that were made, and the effect has destroyed a commonalty that we had long shared. That common heritage of hymnody needs urgently to be restored, and we need to recover a common heritage of language and translations and adaptations.

When the Lutheran Church—Missouri Synod invited the American Lutheran Church and the Lutheran Church of America to join with it in the production of a new service book, the call allowed for a divergence in the hymn collection (of all things) and suggested that, if agreement could not be reached, at least a "core hymnal" be devised. At the very least, in common work between Episcopalians and Lutherans, a core of services might be a way to proceed. But such an approach seems unnecessarily hesitant. It is better to be bold and work toward one liturgical book for two churches that (at least for the time being) retain separate organizational structures but that are clearly (whatever the result of the votes on the Concordat) well on the way toward being one in doctrine and worship and order, in faith and practice. A common book is a clear way of making concrete and visible the level of agreement achieved in the Concordat. It is, moreover, a challenge to each of us to demonstrate to the other the depth of our commitment to unity and to common work. We ought to be two churches sharing one liturgy, even as we in the vision of the Concordat will eventually have one ministry and apostolic order.

As I read the signs of the times (admittedly, a dangerous activity but nonetheless a necessary one), it seems apparent that the era of exclusively denominational concern has passed. A new spirit, a new approach, a new outlook is appropriate at the dawn of a new millennium. The Concordat is the result of years of patient and painstaking work on the part of both churches. Now is the time to act upon that agreement in a bold way. It is, I submit, not enough to agree on organizational steps to integrate our ministries over the course of the next decades and to introduce into American Lutheranism a genuine episcopal polity and understanding. We need a more obvious and public sign of our commitment to the most intimate act two church bodies can engage in—common prayer.

I invite the Episcopal Church to take the title of its service book with still greater seriousness so that it can become truly a book of common prayer. I ask my own church to take up the promise inherent in the title of the *Common Service Book* and in the Preface to the Common Service, "We would gladly behold the day when to One, Holy Catholic, Christian Church, shall use one Order of Service, and unite in one Confession of Faith."

My understanding of ecumenism and the nature of Christian worship impels me to ask if there is any reason why we as separate denominations must work on our own to produce our own peculiar book? Is there anything so distinctive about our worship that we require a peculiar book to support it? Whatever the fate of the Concordat (acceptance, rejection, postponement), can two churches who have had such a vision as the Concordat sets forth and who have presented such a bold proposal to their respective national conventions presume to work on liturgical reform on their own? The answer to all of these questions clearly ought to be a resounding "No." Let us therefore work together on one book in anticipation of what will in God's own time become one Church.

The More Light You Let In, the Less There Is to See: The Barrenness of Michal and the Protestant Flight from Ecstacy

Paul V. Marshall

IT HAS BECOME SOMETHING of a commonplace to say that good liturgy is a life-and-death experience, so decisions about life and death may be a way to begin considering the subject.

A comic once observed that it was impossible for him to contemplate his own death and carry a tune at the same time. It is of great significance that the opposite appears to be true as well: While carrying a tune, it is difficult to think of nonbeing. It is said that the human population is divided into those who have considered suicide—and liars. My own midlife period has not been without physical and mental stresses, and so an afternoon came in the cruelest month of 1990 when I found myself in a bookstore, handling a copy of John Kiley's *Self-Rescue*. I was in part lured by its forward by, surprisingly, William F. Buckley, Jr., with whom I do not associate self-help books. Kiley, trained as both a physician and a philosopher, has significant theological commitments as well. Beginning with neither canned insight therapy nor heaps of empathy, Kiley first offers the person entertaining self-destruction a survival technique based on his observations of neurological function. Later in the book, in advising the smoker and drinker, he offers similar assistance, along with an exercise in the subjective experience of integrity.[1] From the how and why of these "cures" he builds his case for the existence of God, the utility of that belief, and what the universe means.

This is not the place to discuss whether Kiley's science, philosophy, or theology is adequate. I do, however, want to reflect on his proposed rescue from those urges to suicide that arise from the mental experience of existential anxiety the apprehension that life may not be worth it or that psychological pain may not be bearable.[2] The biological bases of consciousness, attention, and memory are only beginning to be understood with anything like precision. Certainly the exercise Kiley offers the existentially troubled person is the front end or "user interface" of an electro-chemical process like myriad others in the brain; his technique addresses the same functions as do psychological and hypnotic pain management techniques. These disclaimers in place, it is time to reveal that Kiley's prescription for dealing with suicidal thoughts is as profound as it is countercultural: Contemplate the other, not yourself. As the simplest of examples: If one focuses on and then pays full attention to the sound of a ticking clock, it is not possible to contemplate self-destruction, and the crisis passes.

Kiley's suggestion would appear hopelessly banal if it were not so powerful and so provocative. The suicidal person is called out of self to the contemplation of another. This may have a number of results. The suicidal person may seek to own, dominate, or use the other, taking paths such as hedonism and materialism. Or the person may find in the new experience of outward attention a call to acknowledge the world as larger than the self, beginning to find a universe not finally defined by anyone's subjective thoughts or feelings. Even more, a religiously minded person may find here a call to relate to God, perhaps even to become lost in God.

At this point, of course, Kiley has taken the reader far from a nostrum for avoiding suicide. To do what Kiley asks is not just to avoid self-annihilation. To pay full attention to what is outside our selves is an invitation to ecstasy. *Ecstasy* is a frightening word. For some it means a yielding to overwhelming pleasure or at least sensory overload; for others it threatens a loss of (the illusion of) control. While it may well involve a feeling element, ecstasy is not primarily about feeling good. *Exstasis* means "to stand outside of oneself;" whirling with the dervishes or fasting with the monks is not the required entrance point to ecstasy. Anyone who has suddenly realized that they have been driving without "paying attention" for the last half hour knows that altered—or better—alternative, states of attention are part of everyday life. Ecstasy is another kind of focused attention. To put it subjectively, the ecstatic experience is that which takes us out of self and leads us to participate in a new and larger reality given from without. In ecstatic experience, the sense of being a perceiver is heightened. But that which is perceived takes us away from concentration on self; a kind of union with the other thing, person, or event is approached, if never fully attained. So, in the religious sense, to court ecstasy is to risk becoming the kind of everyday mystic who can look at the stars and end up talking with, not to, God. It is to risk writing

Psalm 104, lost in wonder at sporting whales, trees full of sap, resolving that "I will sing to the Lord as long as I live."[3]

Something can be learned about ecstasy in general from our experience of sex. Sexual ecstasy, once the hormones of adolescence have subsided, cannot be described in terms of pleasure alone, important as that pleasure is. The physical, the rational, and the emotive aspects of experience are not shut down but combine into something greater than the sum of these parts, as two people experience union. But for this experience to take place, each must be willing to go out from the self, toward the other.

Eros has been much maligned, reduced to a craving to "have" another, to what is commonly called lust. Prescinding entirely from the question of whether lust is necessarily bad, it is enough here to note that eros also has the sense of "unitive desire," and is not necessarily opposed to *agape* at all. Unitive desire was not something the Hebrews were much willing to talk about, and this probably reflects their avoidance of anything that reminded them of the fertility religions around them. Hosea is the only prophet who dares to speak in terms of God's desire for the people, God's wooing of the people. God desires us. We often describe the Trinity as the community of God's love, as expressing God's eternal identity and purpose. Is it too much to argue that God has chosen to be, in some special sense, incomplete without us and that the urge for union with God that Augustine is remembered for describing reflects God's desire (here language cracks), God's passionate need, as much as our own often misdirected desires?

As Hosea and any other jilted lover knows, ecstasy has its price. Its content, however revelatory of the other, cannot be neatly packaged. Its timing and proportions are uncertain. It often produces just as much disorientation as knowledge, and the knowledge it gives is not the kind that is ordinarily reducible to propositions. When religion becomes focused primarily on propositions, as most of the Reformation did, the presence, let alone the courting, of ecstasy is usually de-emphasized, if not absolutely rejected. A German Sunday school song, whose title and source I no longer remember, sang confidently to the effect that even if I never, ever feel or experience anything, Christ's love for me is real and to be trusted. Here many of us learned to discount and even distrust any element of religion that was not related to the exposition of truth and the reinforcement of a kind of "faith" that seemingly rejoiced more in knowing about God than in knowing God. Although there were unquestionably legitimate reasons for the Reformation emphasis on faith and the centrality of the Scriptures, a paradox resulted. The Reformation is often said to have set the individual Christian free. Nonetheless, in its classic forms, it also left the individual alone, isolated in the cold world of teachings to be inculcated and believed. That Lutheranism would spawn pietism, and Anglicanism breed Methodism, seems only natural. The pointed rejection of the Metaphysical Poets by church and academy until this century is not surprising: There was no room for emotion in Cranmer's legacy, unless one counts his very last moments.

When one experiences Christianity with only this forbidding intellectual agenda, there is only now: The past is another country. Horton Davies argues that the reason the Puritans had no liturgical year, the reason they spoke little of even the New Testament saints, was carefully considered. For him, the Puritan refusal to commemorate the past— even events in the life of Christ, let alone events in the lives of the saints —put all the emphasis on present-day sanctification. "Puritans, in their type of spirituality did not, like Roman Catholics or Anglicans, aim directly at the imitation of Christ. Rather they recapitulated the story of Everyman Adam, from temptation and fall, through reconciliation, restoration, and renewal."[4]

The result of this was a spirituality that centered on the subjective experience of one's interior condition, but not as in the classic paths of spirituality. This subjectivity had an ever-decreasing frame of reference, a shrunken field of view. In some cases it became the path to solipsism and self-indulgence, as everything was brought inward, not drawn out. The example par excellence is the American adoption and transformation of the Israelite story of the conquest of Canaan. The settlers read it according to their need to justify taking what they wanted. This inward focus made them blind to the Hebrew prophets' critique of Israel's habitual injustice. They learned nothing from the story; it became simply a warrant to commit the same sins that Israel had. Thus the indigenous peoples of New England were virtually exterminated, and forgotten were the prophetic words about social justice and the treatment of strangers. As this sin deteriorated into a bad habit, the new American nation had a pre-fabricated attitude and modus operandi at hand; western expansion became as unstoppable as the tides.

If we are to re-own ecstasy, if we are to open ourselves to communion with God as we are open to information about God, our theological agenda must shift. To re-own ecstasy is in part to re-own the biblical narrative in both a broad and particular sense. (Seminarians in particular need to know and feel the contours and movement of the biblical story, even more than they need to ponder how many Isaiahs there were.) It is also a call to a renewed sense of liturgy, both as an encounter with the mystery of God and as an act of public service. To seek ecstasy is to be about the business of remaking oneself as part of transtemporal communion, servant and served. Paradoxically, this can only take place if one is focused far beyond anything that might be called self-fulfillment. Yet only in this dedication to communion with others and the Other is there fulfilled a kind of duty to divinization.

PROTESTANTISM'S INCURABLE WOUND

NOT TOO LONG AGO I helped conduct a group of Yale students of liturgy, music, and the related arts on a study tour in England. We were all reduced to tears, or something close to them, when we celebrated the eucharist on the day of Pentecost, using one of the ruined columns of the abbey at Lindisfarne for our altar. In the following weeks, as we moved from spot to spot, one or another member of the group would be overcome by something we encountered. When we came to my favorite cathedral, Ely, it was my turn, much to my surprise, for I knew that we would see both beauty and devastation. The cathedral's large Lady Chapel was once filled with frescoes and statuary, lit by the contemplative light of stained glass. All of this had been destroyed during the Civil War of the 1640s, and I had seen the room several times before with that knowledge, as well as with the usual disapproving thoughts about the worst kind of Philistines, the ones on a mission.

This time was very different, however, for members of the Yale Camerata formed a circle in the Lady Chapel and began to sing. The live acoustics born of a high ceiling, stone and glass, added a nimbus of reverberation to their clear sound. For Anglicans, there is a fourth B in music; before Bach we say Byrd, the composer who marked the peak of Renaissance vocal composition. Now standing in the center of this once-glorious room, with its ruined wall paintings, empty niches, and overwhelming, ostentatious, ugly "plain board" where an altar had once been, I was surrounded by their circle of sound as they sang beautifully and ironically Byrd's *Ave verum corpus*.[5] I had no thoughts at first, only unstoppable tears. In the terrible contradiction between the music's sublime invitation to adoration and the brilliant light of the clear windows' revelation... of nothing left to see, I felt the deep but long-accustomed throb of Protestantism's incurable wound twist into a new, famished, moan that could no longer be suppressed. The room's windows and frescoes had once told the entire biblical story, and its statuary surrounded worshippers with reminders of the flesh in which that story had continued in the stories of saints and martyrs. Bright light is for the scythe and winnowing fork of ideas, not the communion and community of stories, so the stories had to go. The destruction of art was more than a brutal act of Philistinism. The seventeenth-century iconoclasm at Ely was very much like the calculated overkill in the execution of Nicholas II along with his wife and all of their children: No reminder of the old ways was to be tolerated, and no vehicle left for returning to them.

But what good are ideas that can reign only by terror? Revolutionaries never really trust "the people" anyway. Witness musician Zwingli as he banned all song from the liturgy. The British were denied their story, their warm colors, their myth and ritual to some degree by Henry VIII, Edward VI, and Elizabeth I; they were denied them completely during the Interregnum. The result included the rapid growth of Freemasonry and other extraliturgical religious ritual. Read the descriptions of several torchlight funeral processions at midnight in the *Diaries* of Samuel Pepys to get a taste for the bifurcated experience of his day. When Pepys went to church, he never commented on movement, color, or ritual: he was there to hear sound teaching aptly presented, and that is where he directs his attention for the vast majority of the reports about church going. He is moved by the power of ritual outside of church and reports that.

The Enlightenment, of course, brought challenges to religion in general. The reader is no doubt familiar with the religious movements that grew up because of, or in opposition to, the new intellectual climate. The presence of the incurable wound meant that most of those movements went either to an extremely intellectualized or else an extremely emotional faith: There seemed to be no way to have both thought and ecstasy. The Western penchant for dualism can only with the greatest difficulty transcend an either/or situation to reach both/and.

Both sides of the debate occasioned by the Enlightenment were caught up in the questions regarding the "historicity" of the Bible; its quality as the story of our ancestors—told so naturally and wonderfully —evaporated. Even those who opposed the Enlightenment's attack on Scripture were people of their time, and we see much of what little was left of Protestant liturgical life atrophy under their stewardship. The richness of Luther's liturgical piety and the surprisingly sacramental core of Calvin's sense of worship were quickly lost by their heirs. Bible and worship were atomized, dogmas was particularized, and it is arguable that Truth replaced God more surely in Protestantism than ever did the switching of statuary in Notre Dame under the French Revolution and the First Republic.

Classical Protestantism historically distrusts ecstasy because it requires room for ways of knowing or perceiving that soar above (and beneath) the products of reason or revelation. Within the Protestant orbit, those peripheral groups that value a kind of ecstatic experience generally do so in a way that the mainline perceives as anti-intellectual and psychologically suspect. The issue is further complicated in America by the statistical likelihood that those involved in ecstatic religion are not of the more privileged social, racial, or economic groups. Ecstasy brings the threat of rebellion or at least suggests an escape, however temporary, from a life all too much controlled by those whose religion is of the reasonable kind. In this regard, it is intriguing to note that modern churches that cost millions of dollars, with an additional million or more spent on an organ, seldom have memorable, or even good, paintings or sculpture within them. Is it possible that here again the beautiful is rejected precisely because it opens the heart of the onlooker to experiences that cannot be standardized or controlled?[6]

Religions of the head not only lack art; they also lack story. Protestantism's bias against ecstasy gives the human spirit no place to dance, no place to go. When that bias is combined with a critical approach to the Bible that remains focused on what we can or cannot believe (and it matters not which), humanity has no place to be from. Children tend to be told bits of the story but grow up with no sense of a grand narrative. The Bible stands in peculiar disjunction from us, except its moralizing. Liturgy fares no better: with no story in which to situate itself, it atrophies. About the only thing left in Protestant worship has been hymnody, which may well get any credit due for the survival of Christianity in Protestantism.

Religious stories told in a larger ritual setting connect us, have power over us, and, when entered into contemplatively, invite us to ecstasy. First of all, listening to a story is an altered state of consciousness for the hearer: whether the story is about the preacher's childhood memories or Ezekiel in the valley of dry bones, the listener ordinarily goes into a kind of "long ago and far away" mode. Because this is a mild trance state (and we must not be afraid of that word) listeners are readily receptive to the many layers of meaning and suggestion in a story, receiving meaning on the symbolic level as well as the data-giving level. A story has characters, settings, and actions, all of which communicate: no propositions are debated, accepted, or rejected by a judicious mind. This is why sermons on the story of the Prodigal Son, for instance, are never as moving as the parable itself, unless preached with or through contemporary stories. Perhaps it also explains why so few sermons are ever preached about the nearly overpowering stories in the Old Testament, such as that of Judah and Tamar (Genesis 38). But those that are can be blockbusters. Because stories, even invented ones, circumvent the part of us that wants to argue about propositions, they are powerful ways to get ideas and possibilities on the table that would not otherwise be entertained. Because they work on several levels at once, they have power to transform and even to heal, which is another way of saying that they invite us to ecstasy.

Thus evocative detail, voice, and "once-upon-a-time" quality count in a story. Garrison Keillor's "Lake Wobegon" stories, most of which are thinly disguised sermons or morality playlets, certainly could be summarized in a paragraph of facts and precepts. However, they would lose their transforming power immediately, even while retaining all their "truth." I listened once to the story of Ezekiel in the valley of dry bones being retold by a preacher who made us all feel its magic, made us know why and how the Israelites felt dead "and clean cut off." Everything in me that ever felt that way was there with them. And when he got to the rustle of the Spirit and the rattling of those bones as unexpected new life came to visit them and reconnect their broken and scattered selves, I was aware

of how deeply I wanted a full experience of that life. I was ready, receptive, attentive when it was about to be offered.[7]

In the liturgy, stories bring more than information about a past:
They bring wisdom. This is so because the stories told in the liturgy are
paraded by us in their ultimate context, the story of Jesus and all of
human history. This is why the altar once in the chapel at Ely was so
easily and gracefully surrounded by frescoes and statues: The Mass was
celebrated in the midst of the story, and the story was known in relation
to the Mass. When liturgy is story—but is also movement and color and
spatial relationship and sound (which do more than simply bear the
text)—our entire person is transported to a world where other realities
entice us to enter the ecstatic. As the liturgy that permits the ecstatic
unfolds, in our contemplation we are revealed to ourselves as the Body of
Christ, surrounded by a cloud of witnesses, singing at the throne with all
the company of heaven. The "now," the present moment that obsessed
Puritan spirituality, occurs in a transforming context when liturgy
contains an invitation to ecstasy.

Understanding the past as an objective set of ideas and events
about which we might or might not "know" something was only one
part of the problem. The other part was that this attitude also prevented
individuals from knowing themselves as part of a cosmic tapestry in
which they were the latest strands. The result was a kind of alienation or
dissociation from people in other places, times, and races; consequently,
the myth of modern humanity arose dissociated from itself in many
ways. We have known technology; some of us believe that we have
known progress; however, no one argues that the human spirit has
advanced. I believe that our post-Christian, post-ecstatic, post-story
sensibilities are increasingly detached from history and myth and now
also from the things of life, from the earth itself. Our dissociated culture
no longer functions as a weaver bringing the strands of history together,
nor does it embrace any similar myth. For the post-World War II generation, the future became the great threat; as kindergartners in the early
1950s, we had already practiced dying in neat rows in those public
school rehearsals for atomic holocaust called air raid drills. We never
talked about it. What was there to say? The 1960s would let that fear
and anger out in a way that further hobbled society, and as this is written, we Baby Boomers rule the world.

THE LOSS OF STORY AND SYMBOL

TO SUMMARIZE, THEN, the mainline churches accepted rationalism and biblical criticism and believed in progress and modernity. To be sure this sparked many countermovements. Romantic reaction, for example, may well have helped bring the Roman Catholic liturgical movement and its parallels into Anglicanism and, later, into Lutheranism. But these movements betrayed themselves with utterly rationalist or moralistic preaching and teaching. (Nothing induces alienation or sleep faster than a sermon explaining how we should feel at certain ritual moments, regardless of whether the topic is balloons or monstrances.)

In general, having nothing else to say, religion without a story thus took refuge in good works, which, as we all know, never go unpunished. Few people risked understanding what was happening to the soul of the West, and fewer people tried to speak to it. There were early warnings of cultural fission. The first tremendous signals that something was wrong appeared in the "lost generation" of the 1920s.

In *The Great Gatsby*, the protagonist, feeling himself to be out of place in his dour Midwestern Protestant world, is portrayed as creating himself, inventing a name, a past, and a destiny. He had thought that money was the barrier to his acceptance, but it was money and history—a history that, as Tom Buchanan rightly snarls, he could never know. The world that Gatsby thought he could buy into turned out not to exist.

At the same time that Fitzgerald was writing, the young T. S. Eliot sat at his banker's desk, and knowing that the present was ailing, sent out the call for a return to a vivifying past. Whether it is Eliot's young man, carbuncular, idiotically fumbling to make love with a bored flapper, or Fitzgerald's Gatsby, financing an unreal cosmology by bootlegging and bond forgery, both high and popular art are here concerned with the loss of story, of knowing self as connected. Both writers show humanity without a symbolic tool kit for entering ecstasy in the world that is. Gatsby's green light is an intensely powerful symbol, for it is the symbol of the loss of meaningful symbols—the illusion, if you will, of a symbol. Gatsby believes in it because it is all he has to believe in. He knows nothing else. Gatsby doesn't even escape the bleak Lutheranism from which he originally fled: An unsympathetically portrayed, impatient Lutheran minister returns him to the ground, no friends in attendance save one.

At this time, religion has given up on story to a large degree. Despite his many critics among the probable readers of this essay, Norman Vincent Peale made a truly valiant attempt to rescue religion by making it modern and useful. But in doing so, he reduced the mighty acts of God to a set of principles for self-help, way stations on what a later generation would call our spiritual journey, further cutting off resources that might have been available for *communal* self-help in facing the great trials that were about to come.

The horrors of World War II—the firebombing of Dresden and Coventry, the death camps, and the atomic immolation of two entire cities—left people with little to which to cling. The new values of reason, progress, and modernity were largely rejected, leaving emptiness for those who knew no other myth. The entire Western past was rejected with facility by many thinking people because the past, the story, had been abandoned years before by the religious capitulation to the *wissenschaftlich*, the "scientific" approach to religion. That approach accepted an agenda from outside the community of faith, an agenda that predetermined the relative unimportance of its ultimate product. The nervousness that some Anglicans feel about whether or not Rome recognizes Anglican orders pales by comparison with the intense concern theology professors feel about their relative position in university faculties.

If professional theology hastened to legitimate itself—one year's university divinity school spawning the next year's department of religious studies—parish ministry was not far behind. Christian clergy were busily transforming their profession into a craft, a kind of social work. The amazing thing about this transformation was its basis in a logic that began, "I don't know what I believe, so at least I can do good." It ignored totally the question of how to do good. It also created a prophetic stance over against society and even the Church, and thus institutionalized its limited appeal.

Not so with the movement from social work to the medical and psychological model that came with Clinical Pastoral Education, a program that spread with almost metastatic speed through North American religion. No movement is perfectly bad, and "CPE" brought with it a great deal of good. Its negative side effects live still, however, even though the movement is no longer news. Medicine at that time— and this is still largely the case—operated from a model of sickness: How do we treat, and perhaps cure, this malady? The results of transferring an "illness" model to pastoral ministry and to the Church itself caused one of the greatest shifts in ecclesial reality since St. Paul turned the Corinthians' love feast into a church service. Clergy became increasingly understood as counselors; awareness of one's feelings came increasingly to replace other data about events; metaphors of brokenness and woundedness replaced those of spiritual power, transformation, and divinization. Along with the more familiar sight of doctors playing God, we gained two generations of clergy playing doctor (usually with their clothes on). Seminarians, wearing white lab coats or white jackets instead of the somber hues of the clergy, reported "feeling for a change that I really was somebody." CPE theology is wonderfully ecumenical, even interfaith, in its tenets; it could and did demand, however, very little of the practitioner. It moved the focus from the great story, not to the individual story, but to an entirely relativistic inquiry into what one's subjective reactions to the story might signify. "Twelve step" groups would also have an effect on this ecclesiology of sickness, but it must be said that they at least mitigated the illness model by emphasizing "recovery." In any event, the Church was increasingly becoming a clinic.

While theology and pastoralia were trying to hide their spots, while Episcopalians were putting white gloves on their crucifers in new suburban churches and establishing a corporate bureaucracy in New York, and while Lutherans were scrambling not to look German anymore in the service book and hymnal, the rest of the world was scratching at a deeper itch. Something was wrong with the culture: dissociation and alienation. And it was not getting better. Books appeared with titles like *The Lonely Crowd*, *The Organization Man*, and *The Nature of Prejudice*. Books like these reflected the negative self-assessment of the culture and its confession that the postwar boom was filling pockets, at least white pockets, but was not filling souls.

African-American Christians, who had been efficiently kept out of the white Protestant culture and who had preserved the stories and lived and sung them, were at the same time using their religious resources to begin a process that would transform this country's political life. The culture then—and even more, the culture now—tries to understand the civil rights movement of the 1950s and 1960s without reference to religion, and thus it never gets to the heart of what drove and shaped

America's third revolution.

As the book titles recalled above suggest, and as Erik Fromm repeatedly wrote, humans are inveterate meaning-seekers, and if mainline Protestantism had nothing spiritual to say, or no longer had the courage to say anything spiritual, people would look elsewhere. This search, in part, gave impetus to the Beat Generation, to new encounters with Asian religion, and to the first groups to drop out of the dominant culture presided over first by Ike and Mamie Eisenhower and after them by the tinsel of what we now know to have been a war-mongering Camelot. There were many Beat poets, but clear by the Beat prophet was Jack Kerouac, whose novel *The Dharma Bums* was the first great document of "the movement." It takes place in 1955, and includes a loving but real indictment:

> You know when I was a little kid in Oregon I didn't feel that I was an American at all, with all that suburban ideal and sex repression and general dreary newspaper gray censorship of all our real human values but when I discovered Buddhism and all I suddenly felt that I had lived in a previous lifetime innumerable ages ago and now because of faults and sins in that lifetime I was being degraded to a more grievous domain of existence and my karma was to be born in America where nobody has any fun or believes in anything, especially freedom.[8]

Familiar territory now, but the Everyman protagonist, appropriately named Smith, goes on a Buddhist voyage of self-discovery. He comes to love mountains, the movements of his body, real food and clean air. He explores the importance of the central Buddhist teaching of compassion and discovers the necessity of giving up the isolation he sought in celibacy. Halfway through his transformation, we learn

> I've been reading Whitman, know what he says, Cheer up slaves, and horrify foreign despots, he means that's the attitude for the Bard, the Zen Lunacy bard of old desert paths, see the whole thing in a world full of rucksack wanderers, Dharma Bums refusing to subscribe to the general demand that they consume production and therefore have to work for the privilege of

consuming, all that crap they didn't really want any way such as refrigerators, TV sets, cars, at least fancy new cars, certain hair oils and deodorants and general junk you always see finally see a week later in the garbage anyway, all of them imprisoned in a system of work, produce, consume, work, produce, consume.[9]

In 1955 Smith/Kerouac was more prophetic than he knew; as Smith says, "I see a vision of a great rucksack revolution thousands or even millions of young Americans wandering around with rucksacks."

After a final two-months' solitude on Desolation Mountain, Smith knows that he cannot simply drop out but that, upon re-entering the world of people, he will be different. Here is his farewell:

Sixty sunsets had I seen revolve on that perpendicular hill. The vision of freedom of eternity was mine forever. The chipmunk ran into the rocks and the butterfly came out. It was simple as that.... For the last time I went out to the edge of Lightning Gorge where the little outhouse was built right on the precipice of a steep gulch. Here, sitting every day for sixty days, in fog or in moonlight or in sunny day or in darkest night, I had always seen the little twisted gnarly trees that seemed to grow right out of the midair rock....

[speaking to the vision of his teacher] Japhy, I don't know when we'll meet again or what'll happen in the future, But Desolation, Desolation, I owe so much to Desolation, thank you forever for guiding me to the place where I learned all. Now comes the sadness of coming back to cities and I've grown two months older and there's all that humanity of bars and burlesque shows and gritty love, all upside-down in the void God bless them.... Down on the lake rosy reflections of celestial vapor appeared and I said "God, I love you" and looked up to the sky and really meant it. "I have fallen in love with you, God. Take care of us all, one way or the other." To the children and the innocent it's all the same.[10]

Smith/Kerouac had to drop out to do it; he had to use another conceptual framework than that available in a world of tail-fins, blond oak furniture, and the prevalence of the only color ever actually invented not to attract the eye—beige. But he did it. He was able to fall in love with God. To do that he needed a set of myths and stories, a way to relate in body, mind, and emotion to what was beyond himself.

If what other Beats were looking for was God, what they got was drugs, sex, and anarchy: The movement's hedonism was a thin exterior covering a mass of alienation, anger, and fear. As the Beats were replaced by hippies, little of that changed, except that the hippies didn't know that it was God they were seeking.

Some people with the same needs as the Beats, but who had stayed inside the Church for any number of reasons, started recreating things in the Church but without any essential connection to tradition, to the story. Their religion, the environment in which they taught the Baby Boomers' religion, emphasized feelings instead of ecstasy, relationship instead of discipleship.

Perhaps the most telling point of this religious evolution was the rash of people who chose to believe the wrong-headed etymology of *liturgy* as "what the people do" instead of "service for the common good." In fact, the common good was sometimes lost sight of. The responsibility for this turn of affairs can be laid, in part at least, at the feet of strangely schizoid clergy. They had been educated in biblical criticism to the point where the Bible was next to useless to them, except when applying the anger of the prophets to whatever troubled them about America. Instead of biblical story, which they couldn't recognize as story, they turned to "my story," and to this day, many Protestant sermons center on storytelling. However, in this style it is not the Story that is told but incidents in the lives of the preachers, incidents that turn preaching into another avenue of self-expression rather than (the highly desirable) connecting point between our story and the Story. When John Donne said "I" in his sermons, hearers knew that some universal human truth was about to be explored. When preachers say "I" today, there is a good chance that the sermon is about to enter the still, greasy, gray waters of banality.

It is with a story that I want to sum up these thoughts, the story of David and Michal. As the Scriptures tell the story, it is Michal who first loves David, long before he becomes so important. Her father, Saul, who arranges the marriage, gives David a bargain-basement bride-price: the foreskins of two hundred Philistines. A chapter later, when Saul begins to fear David and wants to kill him, practical Michal helps him escape and ingeniously covers up his absence. Her father threatens her with death for her efforts on behalf of her husband, but she stands firm, determined, and loyal. Saul also apparently tries to give her to someone else, and David goes to politically risky lengths to get her back. So for quite a while they had something.

Further on in the story, after some delay, including the death of Uzzah the overly helpful, the Ark finally arrives. David's government and religion are to share the same location.

And David danced before the LORD with all his might; and David was girded with a linen ephod [which apparently was not much]. So David and all the house of Israel brought up the ark of the LORD with shouting, and with the sound of the horn. As the ark of the LORD came into the city of David, Michal the daughter of Saul looked out of the window, and saw King David leaping and dancing before the LORD; and she despised him in her heart. And they brought in the ark of the LORD, and set it in its place, inside the tent which David had pitched for it; and David offered burnt offerings and peace offerings before the LORD. And when David had finished offering the burnt offerings and the peace offerings, he blessed the people in the name of the LORD of hosts, and distributed among all the people, the whole multitude of Israel, both men and women, to each a cake of bread, a portion of meat, and a cake of raisins. Then all the people departed, each to his house.

And David returned to bless his household. But Michal the daughter of Saul came out to meet David, and said, "How the king of Israel honored himself today, uncovering himself today before the eyes of his servants' maids, as one of the vulgar fellows shamelessly uncovers himself!" And David said to Michal, "It was before the LORD, who chose me above your father, and above all his house, to appoint me as prince over Israel, the people of the LORD and I will make merry before the

LORD. I will make myself yet more contemptible than this, and I will be abased in your eyes; but by the maids of whom you have spoken, by them I shall be held in honor."

And Michal the daughter of Saul had no child to the day of her death.

What the clergy of my generation learned in seminary about this story was political history, part of the end of Saul, the transition to dynastic monarchy, and a centralized cult. That is all probably true, but is there nothing else going on in this story, nothing that evokes recognition from us? Many possible chains of ideation can be followed here, but consider just one, a meditation that is shamelessly allegorical and speaks to our tendency toward dualism.

In the biblical story as a whole, husband and wife are united as one person. David and Michal thus can remind us that each personality has more than one aspect. David, not entirely a hero here, rejects his love, his other half, because it apparently would strangle him. Then comes what we can never feel as deeply as would a Hebrew woman: that frightening concept of barrenness, suggesting that all that is rational, proper, and orderly needs the seminal experience of ecstasy to bear fruit.

The tragedy of this story is that Michal—practical, down-to-earth Michal, who had saved David when no one else could—becomes in her unimaginativeness a threat to him. They are both losers when apart.

Rationalism took us so far down the road that we had to reinvent religion in our own image at a time when that image was distorted, breeding solipsism and self-indulgence. We had to invent psychotherapy, also, because—well, we needed it. Here in the story, we see that David and Michal separately are in major trouble. What if David had answered Michal by inviting her to dance, too? What if they had found a way to stay together? What if liturgy could provide both ecstasy and education?

Liturgy and preaching need the context of their wider story, if the Bible and church ritual are to reveal us to ourselves. When the sermon ceases to be therapy for the preacher and is re-understood as an invitation to transformation by participating in the story, elders will dream dreams and the young will again see visions.

The creation and planning of liturgical worship needs to include both David and Michal—both the side of the poet/warrior/dancer and the scrupulous, ingenious, practical side. Musicians and other artists must be invited into liturgical matters as full partners. We need the beauty of the arts to invite us out of ourselves. Just as surely as preaching must invite us into the story, we need to give up the notion of liturgical music as merely supporting the text. Music cannot help but control how we experience the text, the assembly, and ourselves. We ought not hide from or deny that. We need to take the risk of inviting the visual arts into our worship space, whether that means displaying a major work by an established artist or giving space to the challenges presented by young professionals or amateurs.

Does the pace of our liturgy allow people to be caught up in its flow, or does some officious leader destroy its organic unity as she or he announces each part and page number? If we are to have new liturgies or liturgical supplements, they must embody a necessary partnership of reason and revelation, of the ordinary and the ecstatic. Some nonliturgical churches plan with precision the intended high point—the ecstatic moment—of their services. Why would we want to do less? Are we not, in fact, very rich in moments that could call us out of ourselves? It would be helpful if future liturgies were created with this reality in mind.[11]

Is this line of thinking manipulative? No. We have no choice: How we create and execute liturgy will have an effect on people. We might as well work for an effect that is salutary, an effect that brings David and Michal together again.

New Resources: Access without Excess

Lesley A. Northup

> If [prayer book revision] means to open gaps for each bishop
> and minister to consult his own sweet will with respect to
> doctrine and service, and to let in "the views of the people of
> this age," then I say, and thousands of people will say it with me,
> "God in his mercy forbid!"[1]

> Have we in our Prayer Book reached the *ultima thule* in formulas
> of worship and statements of doctrine?[2]

FOR MANY EPISCOPALIANS, the process that led to the 1979 *Book of
Common Prayer* was an exciting experience of renewal and renovation;
for others, it spoke more of chaos and confusion. For most, almost
twenty years later, the "new" prayer book no longer seems all that new.
Nevertheless, the prospect of further revision elicits the same conflicting
responses heard in the 1970s, remarkably similar in every age—as the
quotes above, uttered by solid churchmen of the 1880s, illustrate.

While the Church as a whole may not yet be ready for further revision, the stability provided by general acceptance of the current book
offers Episcopalians, less pressured now than twenty years ago by the
force of extensive new liturgical scholarship, an opportunity to re-think
old assumptions, imagine new forms of expression, and study the
insights both of the past and of today's innovators. Perhaps we can use
this period of relative security to examine, cautiously but with some
degree of daring, the sources and resources that might in the future allow
further enrichment of the prayer book.

CULTURE AND LITURGICAL REVISION

THERE IS NOTHING RADICAL in this investigation of new sources.
Traditionally, liturgical resources have been culled from a variety of

times and societies: writings of seventeenth-century divines; prayers by nineteenth-century presbyters; passages from Hebrew, Greek, and Aramaic scriptures; eucharistic structures ancient and modern, Eastern and Western; various intercessions for—and from—the whole state of Christ's church. In adapting this cornucopia of material, revisers have also accessed the cultures and eras that shaped them.

Today culture continues to shape and inform liturgical development. The "views of the people of this age" are not merely crackpot, trendy fads but the living stuff that forms and informs the meaning and meaningfulness of worship. As liturgiologist Daniel Stevick has commented, liturgy, with no independent materials of its own, has always been "a user and shaper of cultural materials," without which it would have no building blocks. He emphasizes that "this use of prevailing culture is not optional or decorative. If worship is to enlist our willing participation and provide an illumination of our existence, it must draw on the deep cultural resources by which we define our humanness—by which we dream, think, work, play, struggle, live and die."[3]

We could identify countless arenas of human activity that might contribute to such a richer liturgical experience. Some have already been tested in Episcopal worship—Native American understandings of sacredness, for example, or the pentecostal breadth of multilingual readings. Others may still seem remote to most Episcopalians—meditation, say, or charismatic expressions. But even these have clear spiritual value for many in our time, suggesting further study In a rapidly contracting global village, the ritual imagery, practices, and spirituality of voices previously unheard can provide a wealth of resources for liturgical development. Experimenting with this bounty need not be threatening, heretical, or politically correct; rather, with cooperation, it may prove enlightening, edifying, and enriching.

Of the various cultural movements that invite liturgical attention, one of the most compelling and revealing is the development of women's distinctive spirituality and ritualization. It is no secret that for many in the Church, the mere mention of women's concerns occasions an impatient groan or a cry of "Enough!" Many still see even the movement toward expansive language in liturgy as disruptive and accommodationist. Such attitudes have spurred the development of various alternative forms of worship among Christian women who remain faithful but feel increasingly alienated from the traditional parish liturgy. Such women are not apostates or pagans; for the most part, they are involved, conscientious Christians of various persuasions whose spiritual yearnings have led them to investigate more deeply the meaning of being female and Christian and to seek the fullest possible expression of their encounter with the Holy.

Regardless of whether we are personally in sympathy with such groups, the worship patterns that have emerged in them reward careful study. For one thing, women in these gatherings have rediscovered some fundamental liturgical elements that have, over the years, faded in Western worship. Many of these can offer spiritual beauty and bounty as supplements to current forms of prayer book worship.

For another, much of the worship in such groups has bubbled up naturally, without scholarship or the overlay of tradition. This grassroots evolution can offer valuable wisdom about what some worshippers are seeking in liturgy and what elements most closely resonate with their spiritual needs and cultural location.

Finally, it behooves us to attend to the voices of all Christians and especially to the voice of this largest of all the Church's constituencies. Although not all Christian women, certainly, choose to worship in intentionally women-centered groups, many of the insights coming forth from such groups reflect general truths about female experience and can be meaningful for even the most traditional of women, as well as revelatory for Christian men.

The reclamations and innovations of Christian women's worship take place in the larger context of a different approach to doing liturgy than the more static methods with which we are familiar. Ritologist Ronald Grimes calls this ritualizing, "the act of constructing ritual either self-consciously and deliberately or incrementally and editorially."[4] Ritualizing refers to an inventive, active process of creating and living liturgy, rather than just formally "attending Mass" or "hearing the Word." Ritualizing includes appropriating old sources, generating new ones, improvising themes and practices, imaginatively reinventing perspectives. It is a vital, ongoing activity in which participants are also generators, not just passive partakers. It makes no judgment about the value of tradition, but freely incorporates both the traditional and the new.

When women gather to ritualize, their worship may take a wide range of forms—from the more traditional Christian liturgies of many women-church groups to the ecologically centered spirituality of Gaia groups to the reclamation of the ancient figure and worship of the goddess.[5] Clearly, not all these manifestations will be of equal interest to a Christian liturgist. Close observation indicates, however, that regardless of the varying expressions of the sacred in different groups, the worship that evolves when women ritualize draws on a pool of common images, themes, and actions that mirror the reality of women's lives and spiritual yearnings.

I would therefore like to suggest, as a starting point, several challenging insights borrowed from women's spirituality that might serve as conversation points in our ongoing dialogue about prayer book revision.

OF SPIRES AND SPIRALS

AS WOMEN HAVE LEARNED to worship together, they have become aware—sometimes with blinding clarity, sometimes only gradually— that some images "work" and others do not. The most obvious and familiar example of this insight is that exclusively male language plainly does not work for many Christians of either sex. But while women's awareness of the exclusionary character of gendered language has resulted largely from a rational analysis of liturgical texts and their uses, other insights have emerged slowly out of the communal life of small worshiping assemblies. Prime among these is a complex reordering that reclaims horizontal—earth-bound, creation-oriented, experiential—imagery for God, for our relationships with God and each other, and for the life of the Church.

For example, women worshiping together almost always, and with little forethought, gather in circles. Seemingly automatically, women enter a flexible meeting space and begin rearranging the furniture.[6] On the conscious level, this effects a deliberate creation of community, a fostering of relatedness, that characterizes the "new master image" of the numinous that liturgiologist Lawrence Hoffman suggests is emerging in contemporary worship.[7] Hoffman proposes that through natural evolution, community—as the locus of the human experience of divinity—is replacing the older vocabulary of a transcendent, unreachable God "up there, out there."

Worshiping women seem to instinctively adopt this model, though it is certainly not confined to women's assemblies. For instance, the circle, the most common of all symbols in women's ritualizing, denotes the recognition of a new understanding of God as immanent, as modeled more fully in the gathering of the faithful than in pointed steeples, high altars, vertical gestures, and meteorological metaphors. While this relational image of God is already woven throughout our liturgies and visible in contemporary church architecture, prayer book texts do little to encourage it, and we seldom acknowledge it.

For worshiping women, the circle is, not only an image of the nature and self-revelation of God, but also an image of community and, by extension, of the essentially egalitarian reality of Christian life—a product of our baptism. The vertical imagery that we commonly associate with our notion of God, but of the Church, of the clergy, and of the order of creation, speaks against the powerful witness of baptism to the destruction of all hierarchies and the leveling of all inequities in the priesthood of all believers.

Finally, the horizontal imagery of women's worship also implies a spreading movement outward from the liturgy into the surrounding culture, no longer perceived as a spiritual adversary. When women ritualize, religion and culture are understood as cooperative, inseparable, and mutually informing. The resultant liturgies seem to recognize more fully than traditional ones the holiness in everyday life and relationships, in homely domestic activities and objects, in the rhythms of our bodies, in the interaction of church and society. This, of course, is not simply a matter of "relevance" but can be of profound importance as we seek to identify our place as Christians in a post-Christian era.

What, then, might this horizontal imagery offer us as we consider new ways of ritualizing? A few practical possibilities suggest themselves. For one thing, we might consider removing, or at least balancing, the exceptionally vertical language of the current prayer book, which is redolent with such phrases as "for the peace from above," "God on high," "[he] came down from heaven," and "we are built up as living stones of a holy temple." Such phrases are, of course, hallowed by long use. They also, however, perpetuate a vertical vision of our relationship with God that may keep us from appreciating that God is not only the God of the skies and of the extraordinary, but also the One who is immanent in the world around us and in the very ordinary. Special bonus challenge: Can we reimage the concepts of Jesus "rising" from the dead and ascending into heaven (not to mention the bodily assumption of Mary) as nonspatial events, drawing instead on metaphors stressing God's loving action in the world?

A PRIEST FOREVER

THE SAME PROCESS OF FEARLESS RE-EXAMINATION could attend other complexes of liturgical imagery as well. The ordinal, for example, deserves some attention. If one constant theme runs throughout the ordination rite, it is the pervasive call for the priest to be a "wholesome example" to the people. Now, no one would want to suggest that the priest should be a *bad* example, but we can legitimately revisit the traditional assumption that it is a primary clerical duty to image forth a certain kind of life.

We might ask, for example, to what extent the priest is set apart, different, unique? Is the priest ontologically more "perfect"? If so, is this wonderful grace conveyed at ordination, or is it an inbred gift of God? To what extent does this notion perpetuate unhealthy models of authority and hierarchy? Just how helpful is this idea to a priest's ministry? And what about the fact that clergy very often simply aren't exemplary? What do we do, given the ritual requirements and assurances, with clergy who are abusive, larcenous, promiscuous, and so forth? Do not the promises of the ritual almost guarantee the disillusionment of the faithful in light of such evident reality?

From the perspective of women and some other cultural minorities, the biggest problem is that our definition of "exemplary" is socially conditioned and generally very conservative. After all, for some Episcopalians, merely being a woman at all precludes one from being an exemplary priest. Where women clergy are accepted, they are supposed to be married (preferably to another priest), mothers (only through marriage), deferential, feminine, dressed and addressed differently than male clergy.

Even women's bodily processes are suspect and traditionally are ritually unclean. Can a woman priest be a good exemplar, for example, if she celebrates at the altar while pregnant? What if she has a baby while single, even by chaste methods? What if she chooses to have an abortion? (If "Mrs. Priest" decided to do the same thing, would it reflect as badly on her husband, the perfect example?)

Indeed, various behaviors that many women might find to be excellent examples are not always considered so in the Church. Women, for instance, often highly value such activities and paradigms as communal models of parenting, participating in demonstrations or marches expressive of deeply held commitments, alternative family configurations and methods of conception, breast feeding (of necessity, perhaps, publicly), wearing comfortable rather than conventionally "feminine" clothing, and adopting an informal style of parochial ministry.

The point here is that we would have to do a lot more serious work than merely cleaning up loose pronouns and rubrics or jettisoning lessons from 1 Timothy to develop an ordination rite that will be comfortable for or equally applicable to women and others who may perceive values differently than does the prevailing culture.

In women's worship groups, leadership is shared or rotated or sometimes delegated sequentially to those who are best at each function. Questions of moral worthiness seldom arise, unless someone's character and style is clearly disruptive or unhealthy. Images of shared presidency, mutual ministry, and the essential goodness of all Creation moot the issue of whether the person currently leading the liturgy is a better or worse example in her personal life.

While we certainly would not want to abandon a variety of high standards for our clergy, perhaps we could re-examine the language that talks so insistently about the inherently special character of a priest's life. This could open the possibility of more honest, realistic, and effective ministry, as well as remove expectations that do not necessarily represent mutually held notions of exemplary behavior.

A variety of other symbol systems could be examined in the same way. We are limited only by the courage we bring to the task. For instance, we might reconsider the image of eucharistic bread. Some eighteen years ago, when I was commissioned a Navy chaplain, I was asked at my screening conference what I would do if I were in a foreign country where bread was not available for the eucharist. At that time, it was unthinkable to use, say, rice cakes instead, and had I suggested such a thing, I would not have been approved. Now we might think further of what bread really represents—especially as the product of, primarily, women's labor in fundamental support of life. We might consider whether other cultural circumstances (or even our own) might dictate that a different staple food could more accurately and effectively represent the elemental life-giving satiation and community strengthening offered by sharing the Body of Christ.

Certainly, much of the imagery of our prayer book is biblical or otherwise traditional, and to lose it would be painful and impoverishing for many Episcopalians. At the same time, the experience of women who pray together is that to use such metaphors exclusively fails to encompass the experience of many Christians, women among them. If nothing else, it would be an illuminating exercise to look fearlessly at the symbol complexes we have always taken for granted and to consider how they might be expanded to express liturgical experience more fully. This would, however, require a clear understanding of the use of metaphorical language in worship and a recognition that its effectiveness changes as culture and experience evolve.

THE WORLD AND THE FLESH

AN EXTENSION OF HORIZONTAL RE-IMAGINING is a recognition of our earth-bound nature, our connectedness—and indeed, our indebtedness—to the natural world through which God creates and sustains us. This is a logical concern for women, who, in culture after culture, have been particularly identified with the earth, with fertility, with life and growing things, with the knowledge of herbs and medicines. Though this association was, in earlier centuries, considered a badge of shame and sufficient justification for charges of witchcraft, Christian women today often joyfully reclaim nature in a variety of liturgical practices.

One manifestation of this connection with the earth is the use of natural objects as foci for worship. Plants, stones, fruit, sticks, nuts, soil, water: All can be used in liturgies as symbols of divinity, of createdness, of natural necessity and interconnectedness. Such objects are most effective when they can be handled, arranged, used; they are, after all, familiar and down-to-earth, unlike highly buffed brass or silver ornaments, which practically holler, "Don't touch me!" When incorporated into a liturgy, more mundane objects can be starkly moving, as they were in a conference ritual to which members were asked to bring a handful of soil from home: The soil represented, not only the significance of home, but the overcoming of regional differences, a recognition of earth's life-giving force, and an acknowledgement of God's inherence in all of nature.

We tend to associate the use of natural objects with sixties-era liturgical experimentation and may have wished them good riddance. But recent years have witnessed an enhanced appreciation for the things of the earth that probably deserves greater liturgical expression. Our prayer book texts woefully underrepresent the ecological concerns we need to embrace today. This forced distance, this sense that reverencing the earth is somehow not ethereal enough for Christian worship, reflects a gnostic body-soul division and limits our spiritual breadth and our understanding of our place in Creation. If ever there were an issue demanding liturgical awareness and direct action, it is the systematic destruction of the natural world and our complicity in it. Revision could multiply and highlight texts treating our relationship with nature and incorporate more fully the things of the earth, thus underscoring the insight that we are neither above nor apart from the rest of Creation.

A related insight from women's ritualizing is the role that effective healing rituals can assume in worship. With their age-old association with the earth, women also held in the pre-modern world the roles of healers, midwives, and herbalists. Many are reclaiming these associations liturgically, and rites of healing are often found when women gather together. Models may be gleaned from this that would allow a practical updating of the inelastic and formalized prayer book rite for "Ministration to the Sick," which, among its other inadequacies, makes no allowance for personalizing the prayers, does not involve family members and friends, and requires at least two books and a lot of equipment.

Certainly, women have no claim to exclusivity when it comes to revitalizing these services. But perhaps their experience can offer the Church an appreciation of the healing power of God as present within the assembly and of the curative and renewing character of Christian love, rather than the magical efficacy of priestly touch or blessed oil. Women's congregations tend to understand healing as residing in God's love, expressed in the nurture, common sense, and care of the community and in God's provision of healthy and natural remedies—rather than in miraculous moments of supernatural activity. Such an understanding can supplement our current rather thin liturgical recognition of healing and bring us closer to the New Testament experience of Jesus as healer.

Yet another insight into the incorporation of nature in effective liturgy is the use of natural settings for a variety of ritual occasions. Apart from the occasional Palm Sunday procession or weekend outdoor retreat eucharist, Episcopalians keep their worship, for the most part, inside the walls of our churches. But most church architecture, quintessentially vertical and oriented "up there," is ill equipped to mirror the earth-centeredness that can bring a sense of wholeness to liturgy. While we may not want to move the regular Sunday eucharist outside, it might be appropriate to consider how better to utilize the settings God has provided for worship, with their rich lessons in God's beauty, love, and power.

As a singularly wondrous element of creation, our bodies, too, deserve greater liturgical recognition. Partly perhaps because of the intensity and uniqueness of their reproductive role and the awareness it fosters of their own bodies, ritualizing women have begun to re-celebrate themselves as embodied souls, negating centuries of bad theology that suggested that human bodies—particularly, women's bodies—were corrupt and corrupting. Women's ritualizing assumes that the body is a primary source for ritual metaphors and that sensory experience, in all its variety, constitutes the principal channel of revelation and sacrality. The body thus not only provides the chief metaphorical resource for women's spirituality but is also accorded full status as the mediating agent for human experience.

Consequently, women's worship embraces the sensorial: ritual foods should taste good; incense is used freely; dance and other forms of movement are welcomed; touching and embracing are natural and encouraged. Episcopalians, many of whom are still squeamish about passing the Peace, might benefit from an increased awareness of the goodness of the human body, with a concomitant reduction in our reputation as "God's frozen people." We may not yet be ready to shout, roll in the aisles, or dissolve into uncontrollable laughter, we should, for example, be able to observe or participate in elegant liturgical dance without snickering, or to embrace each other joyfully in the name of Christ. Prayer book texts and rubrics might hasten a thaw and deepen the meaning disclosed in the liturgy, if they more adequately recognized the indisputable fact that we are fundamentally embodied.

As bodily selves, we rely upon and utilize a variety of artifacts, homely yet deeply revelatory. Like the use of natural objects, the ritual employment of domestic and familiar items is also a common element of women's worship. Women have increasingly claimed such traditional crafts as quilting, sewing, and weaving as liturgical symbols and enhancements. The growing use of pottery vessels for communion and of banners hung on church walls, already prevalent throughout Episcopal churches, is part of this same movement toward the earthy and the homemade. It represents the offering of the works of our own hands, not just the works of our greatest or wealthiest artisans, using the most priceless materials. As we grow in our understanding of how best to offer our own life and labor, we might also come to a greater appreciation of the worshipfulness of well-cooked meals, carefully crafted fabrics, and skillfully constructed utensils.

THE MYTHING LINK

NOT ALL THE FRESH INSIGHTS brought to worship by women involve the physical world. For example, one common element is a renewed emphasis on narrative. Although Christianity, like Judaism and Islam, takes pride in its claim to be historical and documentable, it is clear that the record it has preserved is selective. Missing, among other things, are the stories of ordinary people, especially women, whom Arthur Schlesinger calls "the most spectacular casualty of traditional history."[8] Thus, storytelling surfaces as a central element in women's worship, which has as one goal the creation of a medium through which women's stories can be told, shared, remembered, and incorporated into Christian history.

The renewed emphasis on narrative reflects several purposes: further recording historical events; imaginatively re-claiming events whose details are lost to us; sharing autobiographies as acts of constructing both self and community; testifying; nurturing myth. All of these have liturgical applications. The pauses for personal intercessions in the Prayers of the People, for example, offer opportunities for members of the community to note, share, and interpret events that help constitute the community's life. While we may not want to set up microphones in the aisles, as has been done in some places, we might also want to reconsider whether this narrative moment should be preempted by clergy reading lists of those who have asked for prayer.

Christian worship must allow for the telling of the story of salvation history, but also for the telling of how each Christian fits into that story and into the body of Christ. Whether it is during the intercessions, in some separate time of sharing and witness, in lay preaching, in re-interpretations of scripture, or in yet unexplored forms, some accommodation for narrative that goes beyond just reading from the lectionary seems critical if we are to recall our roots and the great cloud of anonymous witnesses to them, and project our story as Christians into the future.

CONCLUSION

CLEARLY, CHRISTIAN WOMEN in their own spirituality circles are engaged in ritualizing, as are many other Christians, both in formal congregations and in interest groups. Admittedly, this liturgical strategy can seem very threatening to traditional prayer book worship. But we need only look around us at today's successful religious movements to recognize that adaptive, culturally participatory worship is touching deeply responsive chords in Christians of all stripes.

Perhaps we should ask ourselves what this approach can offer us, and just what we risk by examining our long-held attachment to fixed forms of worship. Do we lose the beauty of the prayer book if we allow non-scripted elements into our liturgies? Must the fullness of all our worship be contained within its covers? How much flexibility can we tolerate? How much creativity can we allow? How much adaptability to local needs and conditions is acceptable? Is liturgical revision a sporadic event, as infrequent as possible, or an ongoing process in the life of the Church? To what extent can we incorporate ritualizing into ritual?

Many Episcopalians will see in these suggestions political correctness run amok or a faded reflection of the failed experiments of the last revision. Many will consider them tantamount to liturgical heresy, a peculiarly Anglican sin but one we cannot ignore. A few points might help to keep the matter in perspective.

• The value of reviewing and investigating these practices lies in what they can teach us, in the dialogue they can stimulate, in the new awarenesses they might foster. These are not necessarily proposals for direct change; they are food for thought.

• In our counterreaction to the stress accompanying the last prayer book revision, we have been anxious to put behind us any of the innovative suggestions of the time that did not actually wind up in the 1979 book. The fact that women have been able to rejuvenate some of these—and with great success—may indicate the wisdom of retrieving them again for further review.

• The culture in which we find ourselves, for all its sins and arrogances, has yet some good within it, as evidenced, for example, in its renewed appreciation for the earth and our responsibility for its survival or its championing of egalitarian relationships. It may be well to consider further appropriations into the liturgy of those cultural elements that we can endorse and express and in which we see Christ.

• Loosening up might not be a bad idea. Decreasing membership and bored expressions are only the most obvious indications that the liturgy as we now practice it may work well at the level of the head but not so well at the level of the heart, and not at all at the level of the body. The most successful worship of our age has managed to effectively combine appeals to all three.

• Christian women's groups have been tapping into a wellspring of ritual imagery, theological understanding, and spiritual meaning that bespeaks the emergence of a feminine liturgical consciousness previously repressed and unavailable for communal participation. Despite any initial reluctance to see women's needs as distinctive, we may gain by listening to the voices of those women who are struggling to remain Christians in the face of what they perceive to be a remote and unresponsive liturgical tradition.

• More radical concepts than those discussed here lurk in the wings, waiting for a hearing. For example, ritualizing women have developed nonhierarchical leadership modes that do not rely on ordination or licensing; leadership is understood as inherent in the community, not in any one person. This seems less radical in light of discussions already under way about, among other things, lay presidency at the eucharist. Even more challenging is the notion prevalent in women's worship groups that fixed texts are, per se, of negative value and that every liturgical occasion should allow for spontaneity, flexibility, and adaptation. While this concept is certainly not new to Protestant Christians, are Episcopalians ready to contemplate the prospect of not having a *Book of Common Prayer* at all—or of having many?

• Finally, we cannot avoid the reality that, in a Church with no formal doctrine, liturgical change may well imply theological change. This has been, through the centuries, the greatest fear associated with revision. The implicit irony is that this natural conservatism has, at times, worked to keep the liturgy behind the theological curve—that is, it has kept us worshiping in ways that actually contradict our real theological convictions, both corporately and individually. Without question, the elements discussed here have theological implications, not least in the underlying assertion that the thoroughly transcendent God of the prayer book must be re-imaged as fully immanent, present, active, and joyfully evident in the life of the world and all Creation. But this does not seem like an idea most Episcopalians would reject.

Liturgical change is always uncomfortable for those accustomed to long usage, always overdue for those who feel unfulfilled. Many in our Church, like a recent correspondent of *The Living Church*, feel we have already gone too far in bringing God close: "I miss that concept of the holiness, the awesome difference between... me and God," he writes, decrying what he calls the "gum-chewing approach" to the divine.[9] Others recognize further revision as critical if, as Linda Strohmier writes, "we want to be engaged, challenged, emboldened to move ever more deeply into the gospel life."[10]

One thing seems certain: Unless we can consider our prayer tradition boldly and imaginatively, unless we can learn from both the most conservative and the most innovative among us, unless we can dare to examine our most unshakeable pre-assumptions about our worship, we are doomed, ultimately, to irrelevance. We can glean much from the women in our midst who are re-imagining liturgy, seeking to express their experience of God and to re-claim once-meaningful ritual elements that have long been suppressed. The richness of the dialogue that can ensue is already enlivening academic circles and promises to enlighten all who enter into it.

Embrace the Happy Occasion: Prayer Book Revision in Light of Yesterday's Principles, Today's Questions, and Tomorrow's Possibilities

J. Neil Alexander

THE WRITERS OF THE PREFACE to the first American *Book of Common Prayer* (1789) noted that the framers of that book could not pass up the opportunity to "embrace the happy occasion." That happy occasion was the result of being a newly constituted church in a newly constituted and fully independent nation. That church was ready to set about altering and amending its public worship, uninfluenced and unrestrained by worldly authority, "as might be deemed expedient" in these new circumstances.[1]

This was a new way of being for Anglicans in the American colonies. No longer an outpost of the Church of England and responsible to the Bishop of London, the newly formed Episcopal Church could readily sense that it had been given the opportunity to continue and enlarge the vital witness of Anglican Christianity without the restrictions necessarily imposed by establishment, crown, and centuries of tradition that at times had as much to do with politics and government as with religion. But making the changes that were directly "in consequence of the Revolution" was almost surely the easy part. For most of the century before the Revolution, colonial Anglicans had been on a clear and steady course of political and social ascendancy. Their influence in the political and economic makeup of the colonies was out of proportion to their presence in the general population. Although the social and political values of their English heritage clearly captivated the imaginations of many in the colonies, those values became harder to sustain as the temperature of revolutionary rhetoric increased and independence became only a matter of how and when. The highly visible stratification of English society gave way in the colonies to social structures that were less visibly hierarchical and outwardly much more subtle.[2] These realities required the Church to envision its future along new lines.

At the same time, breaking ranks with a well-ingrained religious heritage enshrined in language befitting the monarch of a mighty nation was not going to be popular, even if it was seen as desirable. The Preface of that same 1789 American prayer book went to some lengths to point out that this new Episcopal Church did not intend "to depart from the Church of England in any essential point of doctrine, discipline, or worship" any further than its new circumstances would demand. Never mind that the eucharistic prayer of the 1789 book came by way of the Scottish Episcopal Church's liturgy of 1764 and consequently differed from the 1662 English book in ways that some would still consider among those essential points of doctrine. But the social and political turmoil in the aftermath of the Revolution and the uncertainty of the early years of constitution certainly would have caused many to yearn for anything that would seem to ritualize a sense of security, stability, familiarity, and comfort.

In broad strokes, this was the "happy occasion" that, "with gratitude to God," American Episcopalians in 1789 had been led to embrace. On the one hand were those who could envision a new church in a new land that loved, honored, and respected its inheritance but was not captive to it. They saw a new beginning and all of the promise and potential that comes with it. On the other hand were those who sought refuge from the turbulence of the times in the familiar cadences of the prayer book. They saw the church as the one place that could provide a dependable anchor in a sea of relentless change.

Although this was a new way of being for those Anglican colonists who had become American Episcopalians, it was, in a sense, not a new way of being for the prayer book. It is difficult to think of a time in prayer book history, especially during times of revision, when "the new prayer book" was not caught between competing claims, requirements, and interpretations. For example, the Eucharistic Prayer of the first English prayer book of 1549 preserves elements that stand in continuity with the *canon missae* of the medieval Roman rite, while at the same time introducing into the liturgical syntax of Anglican Eucharistic Prayer elements common to the rites of the continental Reformation. It was this same eucharistic rite upon which Stephen Gardiner, Bishop of Winchester, could expound a eucharistic theology that was very much in continuity with pre-Reformation medieval Roman Catholicism, while Thomas

Cranmer, the Archbishop of Canterbury and principal author of the text, sought to defend it in theological terms more sympathetic to the Protestant Reformers.[3]

This is but one example among many that could be cited from the 1549 book, and each of the revisions that followed was no less caught in the middle. Sometimes the middle split along Catholic or Protestant theological sensitivities; at other times the battle camps were divided between those of Puritan sympathies with respect to church order and those who supported episcopacy. In England and Scotland, successive prayer books almost always generated conflict over attitudes toward the English crown. In the colonial churches of the eighteenth and nineteenth centuries, the 1662 English book would bear the gospel of Jesus into some of the most remote missionary frontiers on earth while at the same time restricting the vision of authentic worship to white surplices and Anglican chant. More recently, a contention has arisen over being Anglican without being English. Prayer book revision seems always to have been the arena for debate and great consternation. But a set of guiding principles for revision was widely accepted even by competing parties. Marion J. Hatchett has demonstrated in some detail that the principles of revision enunciated in the Act of Uniformity that established the use of the first prayer book in 1549 can be traced through subsequent revisions both in England and elsewhere.[4] These principles are consonant with that sort of native common sense that has characterized Anglicanism from the beginning. They will, for many people, continue as trustworthy guides for prayer book revision in the future.

The first two of these principles—grounded upon Holy Scripture and agreeable to the practice of the ancient Church—are surely taken for granted in the Episcopal Church, now and in the future. Our devotion to the Scriptures and the inspiration we draw from the life of the early Church are central to our identity. It is difficult to imagine a Church standing in continuity with historic Anglicanism that would not hold both of these among the *first principles* upon which the life of the faith community, not to mention the liturgy, is based.

The third and fourth of the principles—unifying to the realm and designed for the edification of the people—are a little less clear. In the case of the first, unifying the realm was originally a highly political statement. It implied that liturgical uniformity and the reduction of variant "uses" appeared to be a worthy thing. But it also referred to the manner in which a common uniform liturgy would play a major role in uniting the people of the king's realm linguistically and ritually—and consequently both socially and politically. This was not, of course, a new idea. Liturgical uniformity had long been used by popes and emperors as an appropriate way to bring about political stability through the churches. The fact that every age reinvents the idea of liturgical uniformity—and then almost inevitably gives it up—might suggest to us that the idea is fundamentally flawed in spite of its obvious appeal.[5] But for us, unifying the Church, not unifying the realm, is the issue. And a major question concerns the role that the *Book of Common Prayer* will play in that effort toward greater unity in the twenty-first century.

The Episcopal Church in the United States is now into its third century and its fourth prayer book. With minor revisions, the 1789 book served us for over a century before it was replaced by relatively minor revisions in 1892 and 1928 and the major revision of 1979. The realities of the late twentieth century—transient populations, lightning-fast communications, "the whole wide world" shrinking before our eyes into a global village—give us every reason to believe that future revisions will come before us with greater frequency and with each revision looking less like its predecessor.

As a liturgical historian, I suspect I am better at the past than I am at the future. Prophecy is not numbered among my charisms. I think it safe to say, however, that the Book of Common Prayer, like everything else in this transitory life, is going to change sooner and more radically that many of us desire. When faced with the prospect of change, my understanding of liturgical history makes me very cautious. I worry about fixing things that aren't broken. But I worry more about fixing those things that are broken and making them even worse. Revising the Church's public prayer, even with the best of intentions and the greatest of skill, is perilous business that must be pursued with the utmost care, plenty of time, and a willingness to listen to *the entire Church*. Unlike other denominations that have an effective teaching magisterium or a book of confessional documents as a unifying characteristic, we rally around our principal liturgical book. In a practical sense, we place faithful, common prayer above particular experiences of conversion or the details of doctrinal agreement. This means that the revision of the prayer book is about as serious as business ever gets in this Church.

The tradition of liturgical prayer is sometimes spoken of as though it is a body of fixed texts that cannot be emended, the way most people would think about the canon of Scripture. This position asserts that, if you change one iota of the text, you have changed the tradition. The principal problem with such an idea is that it represents a static definition of tradition. It fails to capture the dynamic sense of movement that carries the tradition forward on the strengths of the past to a yet more faithful future. Tradition is an inherently evolutionary concept. To require that the tradition remain unchanged is, not to love and honor it, but inevitably to risk killing it. The Church's liturgical prayer will evolve with or without our help. The only real question is whether or not we will be faithful stewards of that evolution. Toward this end, I want to raise two questions, related to unity and uniformity, that I believe the Episcopal Church must answer as the next round of prayer book revision approaches.

ONE PRAYER BOOK?

ARE WE GOING TO REMAIN a "one-prayer-book church?" Thus far in American Episcopal history, except for periods of trial use, we have remained a one-prayer-book church. Even though a small number of our parishes continue to make some use of the 1928 book or one of its variants, there is no doubt that the prayer book is that of 1979. This state of affairs stands in marked contrast to some other provinces of the Anglican communion that have, practically speaking, become home to more than one liturgical book. In the Church of England, for example, the 1662 book remains officially the prayer book. But for many the *Alternative Services Book* (1980) has become the principal liturgical book of their local parish church. In like manner, Anglicans in Canada, Ireland, Australia, and Southern Africa, among others, have retained a conservative revision of the 1662 English book alongside a more recent book of alternative services.[6]

The history of these churches is quite different from that of the American Episcopal Church, and this may suggest why having more than one liturgical book is less of a problem for them. In each case and for slightly different reasons, the Church of England was either the established Church for some period of its history, or if not established, it was certainly a dominant force upon the formation of the nation. This meant that the 1662 book, intertwined with the ceremonial requirements of the British crown and commonwealth, would provide the ritual foundation for the public life—the civic liturgy—of the nation as well as of the Church. This also meant that the *Book of Common Prayer* was enmeshed in the national identity in a way that it never could be in the United States. It was held in honor by large portions of the populace well beyond those active in the worship life of the Anglican church. Because of this status in both church and state, prayer book revision is considerably more complicated in these "Anglican states" than in the United States, where a virtually opposite situation exists. The production of an alternative volume of services was not only the best practical option for these churches, but because of the more integrated relationship of church and state, the prayer book did not have to carry the full weight of Anglican identity, unity, and uniformity. An alternative to it was easier to conceive.

In the United States the picture has been quite different. As noted earlier, the impact of Anglicans in colonial America was not insignificant, and the 1662 English book without doubt played a large role in those churches and communities that claimed allegiance to it. But revolutionary passion around the issue of religious freedom launched a trajectory that would eventually take the form of a constitutional amendment guaranteeing the separation of church and state. Thus the influence of the Anglican church was never institutionalized here in quite the same way as in most other outposts of the British Empire. This meant that the 1789 prayer book of necessity became a rallying point for the new Episcopal Church without the external reinforcement of its place in the larger society through politics, government, and allegiance to the British crown. Here it was the centerpiece of an experiment in Anglican Christianity not exactly like anything else, before or since. It is nonsense to speak of Anglicanism of any sort without placing the Book of Common Prayer near its core. But in the absence of the social and political fortification that has existed elsewhere in the Anglican communion, the prayer book of the Episcopal Church has had to carry a disproportionate amount of the weight with respect to Anglican identity, unity, and liturgical uniformity. As a result, the Episcopal Church so far has been more reluctant than other churches of the Anglican communion to produce book-length liturgical alternatives to the *Book of Common Prayer*. Books of occasional services, supplemental liturgical materials, and other approved resources have been welcomed by many in the Church as positive enrichments to the standard fare offered by the prayer book. But up to the present time, these are amplifications only, not formal alternatives.

As we press forward in the next trienium or so, the Church will have to sort this out. One possibility would be to get on with the business of complete prayer book revision. This would involve a clear recognition by the Church that the 1979 prayer book is nearing the end of its useful life, and that we need to enter into an extended period of study, trial use, revision, and the adoption of a new book in 2009 or 2012, if not sooner. There will be those who will support this possibility. I don't.

Others will argue for our first truly alternative book. We would keep the 1979 prayer book as the Church's standard book but provide an official alternative to it with complete rites (for at least daily prayer, initiation, eucharist, and ordination) that are fully authorized and approved for Church use at a canonical level parallel to the prayer book. This would be a major departure in the way things are done in the Episcopal Church and a major revision of the *Constitution and Canons* would be required. But perhaps the time has come. I doubt it.

There is a third option that I suspect will win wide support. Although recognizing that the 1979 prayer book can no longer be referred to as "the new prayer book," I would argue that we have only begun to make full use of its riches and that the spiritual formation of faith communities that results from its use is only now beginning to be felt in much of the Church. After twenty years of pastoral use, we have discovered that, like all of its predecessors, it is not a perfect book and could stand some genuine improvement in some fairly critical places. But I believe the Church has other mission imperatives that require its energy and attention at the present time. I am quite aware that in our tradition common prayer shapes our common mission and that liturgy and mission are inseparable concepts for Anglicans. But our present book has inspired and called us to mission in ways we have only begun to explore. We are nowhere near being finished with what *this book* is calling us to do. For a variety of reasons, I strongly suspect that most of the Episcopal Church is neither ready to abandon the 1979 prayer book nor willing to commit the time and resources required to replace it.

In my judgment, the Church is not ready for a new prayer book. But I do not believe that the work of liturgical renewal is finished, that the work of liturgical scholarship is no longer important, or that the hard work that always stands behind prayer book revision should in any way slow down. When the 1928 General Convention approved an earlier version of the prayer book, it did so in full recognition of the fact that liturgical revision and renewal would always be on the church's agenda. That same convention established the Standing Liturgical Commission so that the work of evaluating, enriching, and revising the Church's public prayer would always be on the agenda. Although a new prayer book seems premature at the present time, this in no way suggests to me that we should reduce our efforts in any way. Instead, I hope that we will devote increasing amounts of time to identifying those rites in the present book that truly will need refinement, correction, or even replacement when the time comes, even to the point of entertaining specific proposals for the sake of study and evaluation. Furthermore, I hope that the Standing Liturgical Commission will continue to provide appropriate enrichments to our liturgical fare in the form of additions and refinements to the *Book of Occasional Services* and *Lesser Feasts and Fasts*, further editions of *Supplemental Liturgical Materials* or something similar, continued improvement of the calendar and lectionaries, and with the Standing Commission on Church Music, further expansion and enhancement of our repertoire of hymns, chants, and congregational music.

PRAYER BOOK OR DIRECTORY FOR WORSHIP?

WILL THE NEXT EPISCOPAL WORSHIP BOOK be a "Prayer Book" or a "Directory for Worship"? This is the second question that arises out of the concern for unity and uniformity. In general terms, a prayer book sets forth an established pattern of liturgical texts that are used in public worship according to a carefully prescribed form. In short, it is a "full-text" book; very little is left to chance, and almost nothing is consigned to the personal creativity of the officiant or presider. Every rite possesses a clear structure, but that structure is arguably more implicit than explicit. A directory, by contrast, is more simply an order of service that establishes the way the worship service is going to unfold. It provides only a few critical liturgical texts, if any at all. The ministers of the service must, within certain restraints, piece together the service from extant materials or create liturgical texts that are appropriate to the occasion. An enormous amount of the work is left to the expertise and creativity of the liturgical ministers. Historically, Anglicans and Lutherans (though the latter have used different terminology) have had prayer books, and Presbyterians and other Reformed churches have used directories. Both types of worship books have been sources of both unity and uniformity in the churches that have used them, although the experience of worship has often been quite different.

The 1979 prayer book has already raised this question for us. Several of the rites—the *"Order* of Worship for the Evening," "An *Order* for Celebrating the Holy Eucharist," "An *Order* for Marriage," and "An *Order* for Burial"—though additional to the prayer book forms, are not unlike directory forms in that they carefully prescribe the *order of service*, but leave much of the work of liturgical design to the ministers of the rite. Many parishes find these orders helpful when something different or less formal than the prayer book rites is desirable. Clergy have, by and large, responded to them positively, seeing them as responsible alternatives to the "full-text" rites when pastoral circumstances warrant. The question for the future will be, "How much more like a directory will we want the future prayer book to be?"

Recent liturgical scholarship has devoted enormous energy to the question of liturgical structures. In some circles, scholars argue that the structure of a liturgical rite bears the tradition in a way that is finally more important than the individual texts attached to it. Taking the long view, the relative stability of liturgical structures over against a somewhat less stable body of texts would tend to support this view. Those who strongly subscribe to this way of thinking might well argue for future liturgical revision that embraces the directory tradition as the model: "Set forth a clear liturgical skeleton and leave the flesh and blood to the ingenuity of the ministers of the parish church."

By contrast, others will be no less sensitive to the virtue of liturgical structures as premium bearers of the tradition. But they will be unwilling to let the formation of liturgical texts become a matter of little concern: "Set forth a clear liturgical skeleton and take no chances. Provide flesh, blood, and vestments!"

A third option might combine both approaches: Establish clear liturgical structures and provide a wide variety of liturgical materials, all of which are in the best sense texts of the tradition, approved for use and carefully crafted to be used within those structures. This would be a natural extension of the present prayer book, both in terms of the larger number of liturgical variables already provided and within the use of various orders similar to those we already have. For example, in the Daily Offices we already possess a wide array of biblical canticles to be sung in response to the reading of Scripture. The list of such canticles could continue to expand and include more biblical as well as other liturgical canticles in a variety of phrasings, translations, and meters, to be adapted as local circumstances and musical resources require. Or, the number of acclamations at the beginning of the Holy Eucharist, now limited to three, might be greatly expanded to include acclamations for each season of the liturgical year, for Major and Minor Feasts, in musical and nonmusical forms, and in traditional, contemporary, or expansive language, again as required by the needs of the local worshiping community. The point is that the structure of the Daily Office could require a biblical or liturgical canticle to follow each reading; the text could be chosen from a larger depository of options, all of which have been approved for use. Or, the *structure* of the Holy Eucharist might require that the liturgy begin with a trinitarian acclamation; the text might be chosen from a rich list of possibilities, all of which meet the theological tests of orthodox trinitarian faith. This would provide for liturgical uniformity through both agreed upon liturgical structures and an official body of liturgical texts to be used within those structures. It provides *both* stability *and* flexibility; it respects the tradition of the Church while honoring the particular pastoral needs of the parish.

The 1979 prayer book opened wide the door to greater liturgical flexibility, both by the expansion of options within the rites and by the addition of separate orders for occasional use. This increased flexibility has been positively received in most of the Church. So it seems highly unlikely that, in the next revision of the prayer book, we will retreat very far on the issue of flexibility. The hard decision will be about how far we should go in the opposite direction. I believe that much can be said for clear and dependable liturgical structures. Spiritual formation rooted in public prayer, patterns of pre-baptismal and mystagogical catechesis, and the natural rhythms of fasts and feasts all require dependable liturgical structures if they are going to flourish.

Over time I have become increasingly convinced of the importance of liturgical structure as one of the principal ways we stay close to the heart of the tradition. In the next round of revision, we must pursue the deep ritual structures of Christian liturgy with energy and devotion. At the same time, however, I remain convinced that we must not lose our passion for beautifully shaped liturgical texts: "Direct us, O Lord, in all our doings with Thy most gracious favor..." "Almighty and everlasting God, by whose Spirit the whole body of thy faithful people is governed and sanctified..." "In Him you have delivered us from evil and made us worthy to stand before you." "Time and again you called us to live in the fullness of your love." These verbal expressions of our faith and prayer must never be taken casually. We cannot risk the possible outcomes if we fail to take seriously the power of quite specific verbal formulae to shape the faith of the Church. Before us will be some tough choices in these matters, and we really must have it both ways.

Returning now to the historical principles of prayer book revision, the fourth one requires that the work be "edifying to the people." Originally, this principle concerned language and the desire that God's people be able to hear the Scriptures, listen to preaching and teaching, and participate in the prayers in their own native tongue—the language "understanded of the people." Assuming that we are going to hold fast to this as a principle of revision, we are thereby going to enter into one of the thornier problems we'll face in the next round of revision: language. This includes language about God, language about us, old language, new language, and so on.

Language, like beauty, is in the eye (or in the ear or upon the lips) of the beholder (or listener or speaker). It is highly subjective. Texts that some find quite clear and resonant are, to others, pedestrian and dull. Phrases that for some are rich in metaphorical depth are incomprehensible to others. I have come to believe and honor those in the Church who insist that they really do prefer to talk to God in Elizabethan English. I am equally convinced that, for others among us the language of Rite One is a significant barrier to worship. I know men in the Church who find the patriarchal tone of our liturgical language unbearably offensive. I also know women in the Church who find that same patriarchal language is safe and comfortable. Some seminarians preparing for holy orders are not interested at all in inclusive language for Scripture and prayer; others are interested exclusively in expansive biblical and liturgical language.

In the last decade, I have participated in more conversations on liturgical language than on any other single topic related to the Church's worship. Reflecting on those conversations, I am convinced that most people fall into one of four camps. The first camp claims that ritual language, like ritual itself, is always archaic and somewhat septic—and must remain so lest we lose the awe, the reverence, and the mystery of it all. The next camp believes that language naturally evolves, and if we're just patient long enough, everything will take care of itself. These folks often care a great deal about inclusiveness in the Church but not very much about inclusive language. "When the Church really begins to behave inclusively," they say, "the words will follow, and until then it's all artificial." The third camp is quite convinced that the language of Scripture, proclamation, and prayer must be "fixed" first, and once we're saying everything inclusively, our behavior will soon follow. The last camp believes that, since God can never be fully or even adequately "contained" in human language, our only hope is to expand the framework of our ritual language to the limits of faithfulness in every direction. Folks in this camp concede that some truth exists in the other three camps; the only way forward is to increase, not limit, the possibilities.

I believe that this fourth possibility offers the best way forward because it closes down no options. Those in the Episcopal Church who prefer traditional language will be able to continue its use. I've heard people say that the Church must leave traditional language behind and that those who like it should be challenged to get their spiritual life moving in the right direction. I've heard those arguments many times—and I remain unconvinced. At the other end of the spectrum, however, we must be just as accepting. The folks who are on the frontier of expansive language are not trying to shock or offend or destroy. They are faithful believers whose commitment to Jesus Christ drives them to find ever richer ways of speaking of God, praying to God, and enjoining one another in the life of faith. Most of us, for the time being, are content to live somewhere in between. But both sides goad our complacency, and are absolutely vital if the liturgical tradition is going to edify the whole People of God.

We must consider a fifth principle that does not arise out of the historical process of prayer book revision but is demanded by the ecumenical context of our time. The work of liturgical study and worship renewal since the Second Vatican Council has produced an incredible ecumenical convergence in matters of liturgy, Sacraments, preaching, and church music. The Sunday rites of many churches—so different in past decades—are now quite similar. Common liturgical structures based upon models from the early Church, common lectionaries, and common hymnals across denominational boundaries have blurred many of the age-old distinctions between liturgical traditions. Twenty-five years ago I could not have imagined seeing the senior minister of a Presbyterian Church lead Sunday worship in a liturgical poncho (or chasuble, as we call it)! This is good, very good indeed, and I believe it is the work of the Holy Spirit.

This convergence places a responsibility upon us that is broader than our own internal interests. No longer can we afford the ecclesiastical luxury of pressing forward in the work of liturgical revision without consultation with other worship traditions that share our commitments to apostolic and catholic faith, gospel Sacraments, evangelical preaching, and liturgical prayer. We need not be ashamed to take to the ecumenical table a grateful sense of Anglican identity. But at the same time we must not allow arrogance and idolatry to infect our attitudes toward other people's worship. It is time for us to actively place our liturgical life on the examination tables of the ecumenical Church and to respectfully listen to what others have to say. I recently attended a meeting of Anglican liturgists at which ecumenical visitors from the Lutheran and Roman Catholic churches were full participants in our deliberations. Their presence among us was an extraordinary gift. This sort of ecumenical consultation must be among the principles of revision as we move into the twenty-first century.

In the Preface to her important study of the 1892 *Book of Common Prayer*, Canon Lesley Northup wrote, "Revision of the prayer book is a painful and tortuous process through which the church does no less than to reshape itself and declare a new vision for its future."[7] Exactly what the shape of that future will be is unclear at this point, at least to me. I am firmly convinced, however, that if we adopt—in ways appropriate to our own time—the principles of prayer book revision that have guided us faithfully in the past, if we are willing to humbly place our work before our sisters and brothers in the catholic Church and take seriously their response, and if we are willing to see in *unity* a gift more precious than *uniformity*, then a new vision will emerge, more glorious that anything we can ask or imagine. And ours will have been the privilege and delight to *embrace the happy occasion.*

Endnotes

CHAPTER 1

1. See below, in the discussion of Holy Baptism, the suggestion that the Blessing of the Font in that rite precede the Affirmation of Faith. The order in which the Blessing of the Font and the Affirmation of Faith come in the baptismal rite should be followed at Renewal of Baptismal Vows.

2. Journal of the Special General Convention of the Protestant Episcopal Church... 1969, 332-34. Contemporary language should replace traditional language in this form.

3. "The Draft Proposed Book of Common Prayer: A Roman Catholic's Appreciation," Anglican Theological Review, 58, no. 3 (July 1976): 365.

4. See Thomas Talley, "Eucharistic Prayers, Past, Present and Future," in *Revising the Eucharist: Groundwork for the Anglican Communion: Studies in Preparation for the 1995 Dublin Consultation,* ed. David R. Holeton (Bramcote: Grove Books Limited, 1994), 6-19.

5. H. Boone Porter, "At the Altar Together," *The Anglican: A Journal of Anglican Identity,* 22, no. 4 (Fall 1992), 9.

6. Joseph A. Jungmann, *The Mass of the Roman Rite: Its Origins and Development,* trans. Francis A. Brunner, vol. 2 (New York: Benziger Brothers, 1955), 301.

7. See Robert Taft, "Receiving Communion-A Forgotten Symbol?" in *Beyond East and West: Problems in Liturgical Understanding* (Washington: Pastoral Press, 1984), 101-109.

8. See General Instruction of the Roman Missal 272.

9. General Instruction of the Roman Missal 56th.

10. See General Instruction of the Roman Missal 272.

CHAPTER 2

1. Leonel L. Mitchell, "Prayer Book Revision—Again," 42, no. 3 (Fall 1996): 1.

2. Book of Common Prayer (New York: Church Hymnal Corporation and Seabury Press, 1979), 856.

3. In his book *Admirable Simplicity: Principles for Worship Planning in the Anglican Tradition* (New York: Church Hymnal Corporation, 1996), footnote on p. 37, George Wayne Smith writes, "Prosper of Aquitaine (c. 390-c. 463) provided the origins of this familiar saying with his words, 'ut legem credendi lex statuat supplicandi, I the law of praying establishes the law of believing.'"

4. Augustine of Hippo Confessiones X. Xxxiii.

5. Ibid.

6. Clement of Alexandria Paidagogos 2, 4, as quoted by Johannes Quasten, *Music & Worship in Pagan & Christian Antiquity* (Washington, D.C.: National Association of Pastoral Musicians, 1983), 61.

7. 2 Chron. 29:25-28 (NRSV): "He stationed the Levites in the house of the Lord with cymbals, harps, and lyres, according to the commandment of David and of Gad the king's seer and of the prophet Nathan, for the commandment was from the Lord through his prophets. The Levites stood with the instruments of David, and the priests with the trumpets. Then Hezekiah commanded that the burnt offering be offered on the altar. When the burnt offering began, the song to the Lord began also,

and the trumpets, accompanied by the instruments of King David of Israel. The whole assembly worshiped, the singers sang, and the trumpeters sounded; all this continued unil the burnt offering was finished."

8. Those words that often appear between the psalm number and the beginning of the text, often in the form of a dedicatory phrase or apparent directions for performance. The superscription for Psalm 4, for example, is "For the choir director [or leader]; on stringed instruments. A Psalm of David."

9. See Psalms 4-6, 12, 33, 43, 47, 49, 55, 57, 61, 67, 68, 71, 76, 81, 87, 92, 98, 108, 137, 144, 149, and 150.

10. Quasten, *Music & Worship*, 67.

11. Plato, *The Republic*, trans. B. Jowett (Garden City, N.Y.: Anchor Press/Doubleday, 1973), 85.

12. Ibid., 234.

13. Ibid., 285.

14. See Urban T. Holmes III, *Ministry and Imagination* (New York: Seabury Press, 1981).

15. From the Latin, limen, meaning "threshold."

16. Plato, *The Republic*, 88.

17. Ibid., 87.

18. Ibid., 62.

19. Ibid., 90.

20. Manfred Clynes, *Sentics: The Touch of the Emotions* (Garden City, N.Y.: Anchor Books, 1978).

21. Marion Hatchett, *Hymnal Studies Five: A Liturgical Index to The Hymnal 1982* (New Yorks: Church Hymnal Corporation, 1986).

22. We all have heard prayers of petition in musical settings that resembled art-songs or choir anthems (such as Wesley's "Lead Me, Lord"), but these seldom function as congregational prayers.

23. These are found on p. 286, 333, 340, 361, 367, 369, and 372 of the *Book of Common Prayer.*

24. These are found on p. 529, 541, and 560 of the *Book of Common Prayer.*

25. Galen Bushey, ed., *The Prayer Book Concordance* (New York: Church Hymnal Corporation, 1988), 761.

26. Mircea Eliade, *Rites and Symbols of Initiation: The Mysteries of Birth and Rebirth* (New York: Harper & Row, 1975), 28.

27. Rabbi Lawrence A. Hoffman in *Beyond the Text* (Gloomington and Indianapolis: Indiana University Press, 1989) describes on p. 155 the use of music by yordei merkavah mystics, a group said to have been active in Jewish "antiquity."

28. Ibid., 6.

29. Quasten, *Music & Worship,* 59.

30. Ibid.

31. J. Geffken, "Komposition and Entsehungszeit der Oracula Sibyllina" (Leipzig: 1902), 38, quoted in Quasten, *Music & Worship,* 60.

32. Catherine M. Wallace, "Faith and Fiction: Literature as Revelation," *The Anglican Theological Review* 78, no. 3 (Summer, 1996): 382.

33. For further information about the Leadership Program, telephone the program's coordinator/consultant, Marti Rideout, at (703) 250-6757.

34. Bexley Hall in Rochester, New York, offers a master of divinity with concentration in Pastoral Music. Call Carol Doran at (716) 381-3189 for further information.

35. Isa. 30:29.

CHAPTER 3

1. Richard Hooker, *Of the Lawes of Ecclesiastical Polity*, I. xvi, 8.

2. Daniel Stevick, author of the last major textbook on canon law in the Episcopal Church (published more than thirty years ago), remarked in his introductory comments that most Episcopalians (including the majority of clergy) had little or no awareness of any but the most basic precepts of canon law and even less interest. *Canon Law: A Handbook* (New York: Seabury Press, 1965), vii-xi passim. But see Francis Helminski, "Our Legal Tradition Needs Revival," *The Living Church* 5 (January 1997): 17.

3. Stevick remarked of the Episcopal Church of the 1960s that "where the [canon law] tradition is kept alive, it tends to be carried on by parsons of curious learning and a tendency to pettifoggery—regarded by their parishioners and associates with patient amusement." Ibid., viii.

4. The Ludlow Professorship of Ecclesiastical Polity and Law was established at the General Theological Seminary in the 1860s. Francis Vinton was the first nominated to the chair; his nomination was ratified by the seminary's trustees in 1869. The last to hold the Ludlow chair was Ralph B. Pomeroy; elected professor in 1919, he resigned in 1925. Thereafter, polity and canon law were taught by John Alexander Richardson until 1945 and by Walter Herbert Stowe from 1945 to 1946. Curriculum changes gradually absorbed polity into church history and the pastoral aspects of canon law were taught as part of course work in parochial administration. The Ludlow Professorship has not been filled since Pomeroy. Powel Mill Dawley, *The Story of the General Theological Seminary* (New York: Oxford University Press, 1969), 220,320,367.

5. Ladislas Örsy, *Theology and Canon Law: New Horizons for Legislation and Interpretation* (Collegeville, Minn.: Liturgical Press, 1992), 11. Many of Örsy's articles have been revised and reprinted in this collection. However, his article "Lonergan's Cognitional Theory and Foundational Issues in Canon Law: Method, Philosophy, and Law, Theology and Canon Law," *Studia Canonica 13* (1979): 177-244, is essential to understanding Örsy's development of the epistemological context for his hermeneutic.

6. Örsy, Theology, 14.

7. Ibid., 12.

8. Ibid., 15. Örsy argues that this shift has been completed by the Roman church. Others may be less sanguine about its true success in adopting a new attitude of mind, as Paul VI suggested, particularly with regard to any permanent shift in self-understanding from imperium to communio.

9. Ibid., 30.

10. Ibid., 15.

11. Örsy adopts and develops Bernard Lonergan's doctrine of horizon, arguing that "mental operations and their results in human persons are essentially dependent on and limited by their field of vision." Rooted in human experience, we test horizons by both self-observation and through observing others. Horizon enables us to comprehend not only the process by which we acquire knowledge but how we communicate ideas to others. Cautioning that language can sound the same from one horizon to another while meanings may differ, Örsy suggests that "to establish communications, the horizons should be adjusted first, and the exchange of ideas should follow." See Örsy, Theology, 19-20 and 23-24.

12. Ibid., 34.

13. Ibid.

14. Örsy's fifteen rules of interpretation were inspired by the regulae juris of Boniface VIII. See Örsy, *Theology*, 77. These rules of canonical interpretation have also been interpreted by liturgical scholar John Huels, *One Table, Many Laws: Essays on Catholic Eucharistic Practice* (Collegeville, Minn.: Liturgical Press, 1986), 19-33.

15. Thomas Richstatter, "Changing Styles of Liturgical Law," *The Jurist 38* (1978): 419-25 passim.

16. "...it will also appear that this Church is far from intending to depart from the Church of England in any essential point of doctrine, discipline, or worship; or further than local circumstances require." *Book of Common Prayer* (New York: Church Hymnal Corporation, 1979), 9-11.

17. "A Book of Common Prayer, Administration of the Sacraments, and other Rites and Ceremonies of the Church, Articles of Religion, and a form and manner of making, ordaining, and consecrating Bishops, Priests, and Deacons, when established by this or a future General Convention, shall be used in the Protestant Episcopal Church in those States, which shall have adopted this Constitution." *Constitution and Canons of the Protestant Episcopal Church in the United States of America* (Boston: John & Thomas Fleet, 1800), 8.

18. Now Article X. See *Constitution and Canons for the Government of the Protestant Episcopal Church in the United States of America Otherwise Known as the Episcopal Church.* Adopted in General Conventions 1789-1994 (New York: Episcopal Church Center, 1994), 8.

19. Örsy, Theology, 33.

20. Ibid., 51.

21. Ibid., 77.

22. Bernard Lonergan, *Method in Theology* (New York: Herder and Herder, 1972), xi. Although a Jesuit, Lonergan's method has both applicability and appeal in a broader, non-Roman Catholic, context. Anglican

theologian Taylor Stevenson has argued persuasively that Lonergan's transcendental method "is the method which is implicitly and usually unselfconsciously at work in Anglican theology." See W. Taylor Stevenson, "Is There a Characteristic Anglican Theology?" in *The Future of Anglican Theology,* ed. M. Darrol Bryant (New York: Edwin Mellen Press, 1984), 21.

23. Örsy, *Theology,* 10, citing Canon Law Digest 8:105.

CHAPTER 4

1. Edward Yarnold, S. S., *The Awe-Inspiring Rites of Initiation: Baptismal Homilies of the Fourth Century,* Slough, England: St. Paul Publications, 1971, ix.

CHAPTER 5

1. Timothy Jack Ward, "Inclusive, in Design and Worship," *New York Times* (April 4, 1996): C1.

2. F. L. Cross and E. A. Livingstone, eds., *Oxford Dictionary of the Christian Church* (New York: Oxford Univ. Press, 1974), 254.

3. Nathan Mitchell, *Cult and Controversy* (New York: Pueblo Press, 1982), 21.

4. Norman Perrin, *Rediscovering the Teaching of Jesus* (New York: Harper & Row, 1967), 107-108.

5. John Koenig, *New Testament Hospitality* (Collegeville, Minn.: Liturgical Press, 1988), 2.

6. Krister Stendahl, *Paul Among Jews and Gentiles* (Philadelphia: Fortress Press, 1976), 58.

7. Stendahl, *Paul Among Jews,* 67.

8. Gregory Dix, *The Shape of the Liturgy* (New York: Seabury Press, 1945), 17.

9. Ibid., 41.

10. Ibid., 356n.

11. Laurence Hull Stookey, *Baptism: Christ's Act in the Church* (Nashville: Abingdon Press, 1982), 79.

12. *The Doctrine of the Twelve Apostles* (London: SPCK, 1922), 29.

13. Dix, Gregory, ed. *The Treatise on the Apostolic Tradition of St. Hippolytus of Rome,* rev. ed. Henry Chadwick, (Conn.: Morehouse Publishing, 1992), 46.

14. *The Apostolic Tradition,* 58.

15. E. C. Whitaker, "Baptism," *In Essays on Hippolytus,* ed. Geoffrey Cuming, Grove Liturgical Study no. 15, (Braincote: Grove Books, 1978), 52.

16. Gordon W. Lathrop, *Holy Things* (Minneapolis: Fortress Press, 1993), 63.

17. Stookey, *Baptism,* 72.

18. Ibid., 73.

19. Leonel L. Mitchell, *Praying Shapes Believing* (Wilton, Conn.: Morehouse Publishing, 1985), 116.

20. Alexander Schmemann, *The Eucharist* (New York: St. Vladimir's Press, 1988), 144.

21. Schmemann, *Eucharist,* 144.

22. Ibid., 147.

23. Ibid., 145.

24. Ibid., 142.

25. Ibid., 153.

26. Michael Merriman, *The Baptismal Mystery and the Catechumenate* (New York: Church Hymanl Corporation, 1990), 35.

CHAPTER 6

1. *The Church of South India, The Book of Common Worship* as authorised by the Synod 1962 (London: Oxford University Press,1962).

2. The Standing Liturgical Commission of the Episcopal Church, *The Ordination of Bishops, Priests, and Deacons,* Prayer Book Studies, no. 20 (New York: Church Hymnal Corporation, 1970), 19-22, 33-34.

3. Ibid., 33-34.

4. *Book of Common Prayer* (New York: Church Hymnal Corporation, 1979), 513.

5. The Anglican Church of Canada, *The Book of Alternative Services of the Anglican Church of Canada* (Toronto: Anglican Book Centre, 1985), 634.

6. BCP 79, 543.

7. Paul F. Bradshaw, *The Anglican Ordinal: Its History and Development from the Reformation to the Present Day,* Alcuin Club Collections, no. 53 (London: SPCK for the Alcuin Club, 1971), 26-29.

8. BCW (1962), 177.

9. The Church of the Province of New Zealand/Te Haahi o te Porowini o Niu Tireni, *A New Zealand Prayer Book*/He KarakiaMihinare o Aotearoa (Auckland: William Collins Publishers, 1989), 920.

10. Prayer Book Studies, no. 20, 89-92.

11. BCW (1962), 164, 170, 177; NZ (1989), 896, 907, 920; Scottish Episcopal Church, *Scottish Ordinal 1984* (Edinburgh: General Synod of the Scottish Episcopal Church, 1984), 2-6, 9-12.

12. These categories are taken from Paul F. Bradshaw, "The Use of the Bible in Liturgy: Some Historical Perspectives," *Studia Liturgica 22* (1992): 35-52.

13. Ibid., 41.

14. Ibid., 41-42.

15. Ibid., 42.

16. Ibid., 43.

17. BCP 79, 515.

18. In Luke's Gospel, Jesus' reading of and commentary on Isa. 61.1-8 is a revelation of his messianic identity. Isa. 42.1-9, the so-called First Servant Song, has generated strong scholarly debate as to whether the Servant is an individual or the nation of Israel.

19. Cf. *The Oxford New Annotated Bible*, "Hymn celebrating God's kingship."

20. Cf. *The Oxford New Annotated Bible*, "Thanksgiving for deliverance from trouble, together with a prayer for help."

21. BCP 79, 517.

22. 1 Pet. 2:9-10.

23. Matt. 28:1-8.

24. John 11:1-40.

25. Acts 16:11-15.

26. Acts 17:32, 18:4.

27. Rom. 16:1-16.

28. BAS (1985), 633.

29. NZ (1989), 917-19.

30. Ibid., 917.

31. Ibid., 918.

32. BCP 79, 517.

33. Ibid., 518.

34. Ibid., 518.

35. *Prayer Book Studies*, no. 20, 26.

36. BCP 79, 520-21.

37. *Prayer Book Studies*, no. 20, 29.

38. Ibid.

39. In Psalm 1, for example, the 1928 reading "Blessed is the man" becomes "Happy are they" in the 1979 psalter. However, in Psalm 8, the 1928 reading "What is man, that thou art mindful of him?" remains fundamentally unchanged in 1979; "What is man that you should be mindful of him?"

40. NZ (1989), 896-97, 908, 920-21.

41. Central Board of Finance of the Church of England, *Alternative Service Book 1980* (Oxford: Oxford University Press, 1980; Oxford: A. R. Mowbray, 1980), 393; BAS (1985), 638-39. In the Canadian rite, the prayer is identical to the English rite save only in the last sentence, which, in the Canadian rite, reads as follows: "And now we give you thanks that you have called this your servant to share this ministry entrusted to your Church."

42. *Occasional Celebrations of The Anglican Church of Canada* (Toronto: Anglican Book Centre, 1992), 119-20.

43. NZ (1989), 921.

44. Ibid., 897, 908, 921.

45. Ibid., 897.

46. Ibid., 908.

47. Ibid., 921.

48. BCP 79, 308.

CHAPTER 7

1. Ormonde Plater, *Many Servants: An Introduction to Deacons* (Boston: Cowley Publications, 1991), 3-4. For a practical guide, see Ormonde Plater, *Deacons in the Liturgy* (Harrisburg, Pa.: Morehouse Publishing, 1992).

2. This basic structure of the eucharist, augmented by gathering and leaving actions, was proposed by the International Anglican Liturgical Consultation V [IALC], "Consultation on the Eucharist" (Dublin, 1995), III.

3. Some years ago Deacon Phina Borgeson suggested the sheep dog metaphor. She recalls: "I developed a three-fold allegory based on sheep-

herding practices in Nevada—with deacons as the dogs, presbyters as ewes and old withers (the natural leaders of the flock-young bucks, aka rams, may lead, but they often lead a small section of the flock astray), and bishops as the sheepherder's pony or horse." Phina Borgeson to Ormonde Plater, 23 October, 1996.

4. John N. Collins, *Diakonia: Reinterpreting the Ancient Sources* (New York and Oxford: Oxford University Press, 1990).

5. IALC, II.6.

6. For these and other possible candidates, see Ormonde Plater, ed., *Calendar of Deacon Saints*, monograph 5 (Providence, R.I.: North American Association for the Diaconate, 1991).

7. In this context "other baptized persons" obviously means lay persons, whose baptism equips them to be assigned as ministers in these functions.

8. See, for example, the Sunday and festal intercessions I post every week at http://www.concentric.net/~oplater1/opprayer.htm.

9. IALC, III.3, with the first two topics reversed.

10. The Canadian Book of Alternative Services has no such liturgy.

11. The key phrase, "God now calls you to a special ministry of servant-hood directly under your bishop," is adapted from the extraliturgical comment of Hippolytus in *Apostolic Tradition:* "[a deacon] is ordained not to the priesthood but to the servanthood of the bishop."

12. See Richard G. Leggett, "'Gentle as a Dove, Living, Burning as Fire: Images and Language in the 1979 Ordinal," in *A Prayer Book for the 21st Century*, ed. Ruth A. Meyers (New York: Church Hymnal Corporation, 1996).

13. Among other sources, this prayer is based on ordination prayers in *Apostolic Tradition of Hippolytus*, early third century in Rome; *Apostolic*

Constitutions, a Syrian document of the late fourth century; *1979 Book of Common Prayer of the Episcopal Church;* and *A New Zealand Prayer Book of 1989.* The language reflects modern translations of Scripture, especially the ICEL version of Psalms 33 and 147.

14. See Paul F. Bradshaw, "The Shape of the Ordination Liturgy," in *A Prayer Book for the 21st Century.*

15. A similar phrase was used in an ordination in the Anglican Diocese of Toronto on 18 September 1996. J. C. Fricker to Ormonde Plater, 20 September 1996.

CHAPTER 8

1. "Preface to the Common Service, 1888," *The Common Service Book* (Philadelphia: Board of Publication of the United Lutheran Church in America, 1918), 307.

2. *Luther's Works 53* (Philadelphia: Fortress Press, 1965), 22.

3. Luther D. Reed, *The Lutheran Liturgy,* rev. ed. (Philadelphia: Muhlenberg Press, 1960), 129-30.

4. Reed, *Lutheran Liturgy,* 130.

5. "Preface to the Common Service, 1888," *Common Service Book,* 307. But see R.T. Beckwith, "Thomas Cranmer and the Prayer Book," *The Study of Liturgy,* ed. Cheslyn Jones, Geoffrey Wainwright, Edmund Yarnold, and Paul Bradshaw (New York: Oxford Univ. Press, 1992), 102-103: "The once-popular view that the 1549 Prayer Book reflected Cranmer's true mind, and that the changes for the worse made under the malign influence of continental Protestantism, is today very hard to maintain."

6. See Christopher Hill, "Existing Agreements between Our Churches," in *Together in Mission and Ministry: The Porvoo Common Statement with Essays on Church and Ministry in Northern Europe* (London: Church

House Publishing, 1993), 53-58.

7. The Lutheran churches of Denmark and Latvia have not yet signed the accord.

8. *The Meissen Agreement: Texts* (London: Council for Christian Unity of the Church of England, 1992).

9. For a fuller summary of European relationships, see Gunther Gassman, "The 1997 Ecumennical Decisions of the ELCA: Their Wider Ecumenical Context," Dialog 35:2 (Spring 1996): 141-42.

10. Philip H. Pfatteicher, *Commentary on the Lutheran Book of Worship: Lutheran Liturgy in Its Ecumenical Context* (Minneapolis: Augsburg Fortress, 1990), 512; "Still to be Tried," *Lutheran Forum* 24:4 (Advent 1993): 24.

11. The author was a member of the Liturgucal Text Committee, one of three representatives of the Lutheran Church in America. The other drafting committees were liturguical Music, Hymn Text, and Hymn Music.

12. We have huge and perplexing issues to come to terms with—principally the language of worship and "naming God"—before any book will be acceptable to more than a small part of the churches. But we need to address these concerns together and share our perplexities, experiences, and ideas.

13. Pfatteicher, *Commentary*, 512.

14. For example, the *Church Book of 1868* and the text edition (1919) of the *Common Service Book.*

15. *The Book of Concord*, ed. Theodore G. Tappert et al. (Philadelphia: Muhlenberg Press, 1959).

16. Carl E. Braaten, "Theology for the Third Millennium," A Report from the Center [for Catholic and Evangelical Theology] (Summer 1996): 3.

17. See my examination of the differences between those who express their faith by a liturgy and those who express it in a book of confessions: "Doxology: Right Praise and Right Doctrine," forthcoming in the *Sewanee Theologial Review,* (1997).

18. By my count each book has thirty-five commemorations peculiar to its tradition in addition to those that are on both calendars; moreover the Lutheran book commemorates an additional fifteen people of traditions other than Lutheran or Anglican who have lived since the Reformation.

CHAPTER 9

1. John Cantwell Kiley, *Self-Rescue* (New York: McGraw-Hill, 1977).

2. The reader is doubtless aware that depression, suicidal or otherwise, is increasingly understood as a biological phenomenon related to the brain's ability to produce and absorb certain chemicals and can also be iatrogrenic when medications are inappropriately administered, mixed, monitored. However, suicide is such a decisive act that it is not associated with all experiences of depression.

3. Dated, as it precedes most current research into brain biology, but nontheless very helpful is Paul Tillich, *Systematic Theology* (Chicago: University of Chicago Press, 1951 63) , vol. 1, 111 ff., and vol. 3, 114 ff. Not as dependent on psychology and hence more enduring is Evelyn Underhill's *Practical Mysticism: A Little Book for Normal People* (London: Dent, 1940).

4. Horton Davies, *The Worship of the American Puritans,* 1629-1730 (NewYork: Peter Lang, 1990), 41.

5. The temporary popularity of a substitute "translation" that began "Jesus, Lamb of God" cannot be discussed here but should be noted.

6. As I have written elsewhere, Sallman's Head of Christ and similar art produced in strict obedience to the canons of commercial portrait and

advertising art, are safe because their message and form are so standardized.

7. I have explored this thought more thoroughly in *Preaching for the Church Today: The Skill, Prayer, and Art of Sermon Preparation* (New York: Church Hymnal Corporation, 1990).

8. Jack Kerouac, *The Dharma Bums* (New York: Viking, 1958), 33.

9. Ibid., 97.

10. Ibid., 244.

11. I have been through the papers of the 1979 revision in their home in the archives of the Episcopal Church in Austin, Texas. It is fairly clear that concerns other than identifying moments for ecstasy in the new rite captivated the Standing Liturgical Commission.

CHAPTER 10

1. H. W. Spaulding, "Enriching the Liturgy," *Churchman* (14 May 1881): 544.

2. J. B. Wasson, "Enriching the Liturgy," *Churchman* (2 April 1881): 376.

3. Daniel B. Stevick, "Culture: The Beloved Antagonist," *Worship 69*, no. 4 (July 1995): 209-210.

4. Ronald L. Grimes, *Reading, Writing, and Ritualizing: Ritual in Fictive, Liturgical, and Public Places* (Washington: Pastoral Press, 1993), 5.

5. References to the goddess and to the beauty of women's bodies raised quite a stir in the aftermath of the 1993 women's "Re-imagining" conference in Minneapolis.

6. Liturgiologist Mary Collins notes that this is the natural outgrowth of

the church jobs women have traditionally been allowed—sacristans, altar guild members. Thus, she claims, they "began by dealing with the familiar. No longer acceptable relationships were reordered symbolically by choreographing new spatial arrangements." "An Adventuresome Hypothesis: Women as Authors of Liturgical Change," *Proceedings of the North American Academy of Liturgy* (1993): 46.

7. Lawrence A. Hoffman, *Beyond the Text: A Holistic Approach to Liturgy* (Bloomington: Indiana Univ. Pres, 1987), 164-71.

8. Arthur M. Schlesinger, "Introduction," in Joanna L. Stratton, *Pioneer Women: Voices from the Kansas Frontier*, Touchstone (New York: Simon and Schuster, 1981), 11.

9. David Meade Bercaw, Letter to the Editor, *The Living Church* 210, no. 21 (21 May 1995): 4.

10. Linda Strohmier, "Does the Prayer Book Need Revision?" *Episcopal Life*, Forum (March 1995): 16.

CHAPTER 11

1. *The Preface to the Book of Common Prayer, 1789.* First published at Philadelphia in October 1789 and reprinted in subsequent revisions of the prayer book in 1892, 1928, and 1979.

2. For the best exposition of these dynamics, with great sensitivity to the role of religion, see Gordon S. Wood, *The Radicalism of the American Revolution* (New York: Alfred A. Knopf, 1992).

3. An Answer Unto A Crafty and Sophistical Cavillation devised by M. Stephen Gardiner, in *Writings and Disputations of Thomas Cranmer Relative to the Sacrament of the Lord's Supper*, ed. John Edmuch Cox for the Parker Society (Cambridge: University Press, 1844).

4. Marion J. Hatchett, "The Anglican Liturgical Tradition," in *The*

Anglican Tradition, ed. Richard Holloway (Harrisburg, Pa.: Morehouse, 1984), 47-77.

5. In the Episcopal Church, William Augustus Muhlenberg seems to have been among the first to have detected this flaw. See Paul V. Marshall, "William Augustus Muhlenberg's Quiet Defection from Liturgical Uniformity," *Anglican Episcopal History* 64:2 (1995): 148-72.

6. The Book of Alternative Services of the Anglican Church of Canada, 1985; *Alternative Prayer Book 1984* according to the Use of the Church of Ireland; *A Prayer Book for Australia* for use together with the *Book of Common Prayer* (1662) and *An Australian Prayer Book* (1978); and *An Anglican Prayer Book 1989* of the Church of the Province of Southern Africa.

7. Lesley Armstrong Northup, *The 1892 Book of Common Prayer,* Toronto Studies in Theology 65 (Lewiston, N.Y.: Edwin Mellen Press, 1993), ii.